How to
Critique
Journal Articles
in the
Social Sciences

In memory of my father, Robert E. Harris

How to Critique Journal Articles in the Social Sciences

Scott R. Harris
Saint Louis University

Los Angeles | London | New Delhi
Singapore | Washington DC

Los Angeles | London | New Delhi
Singapore | Washington DC

FOR INFORMATION:

SAGE Publications, Inc.
2455 Teller Road
Thousand Oaks, California 91320
E-mail: order@sagepub.com

SAGE Publications Ltd.
1 Oliver's Yard
55 City Road
London, EC1Y 1SP
United Kingdom

SAGE Publications India Pvt. Ltd.
B 1/I 1 Mohan Cooperative Industrial Area
Mathura Road, New Delhi 110 044
India

SAGE Publications Asia-Pacific Pte. Ltd.
3 Church Street
#10–04 Samsung Hub
Singapore 049483

Acquisitions Editor: Vicki Knight
Editorial Assistant: Jessica Miller
Production Editor: Brittany Bauhaus
Copy Editor: Pam Schroeder
Typesetter: Hurix Systems Pvt. Ltd.
Proofreader: Rae-Ann Goodwin
Indexer: Diggs Publication Services, Inc.
Cover Designer: Anupama Krishnan
Marketing Manager: Nicole Elliott
Permissions Editor: Karen Ehrmann

Printed in the United States of America

Library of Congress Cataloging-in-Publication Data

Harris, Scott R., 1969 September 16-

How to critique journal articles in the social sciences /
Scott R. Harris.

pages cm

Includes bibliographical references and index.

ISBN 978-1-4522-4134-0 (pbk. : alk. paper) –
ISBN 978-1-4833-1193-7 (web pdf) –
ISBN 978-1-4833-2291-9 (epub)
1. Social sciences–Research— Evaluation. 2. Social
science literature. 3. Criticism. I. Title.

H62.H2565 2013

808.06'63–dc23

2013031336

This book is printed on acid-free paper.

13 14 15 16 17 10 9 8 7 6 5 4 3 2 1

BRIEF CONTENTS

DETAILED CONTENTS

PREFACE

Journal articles are the bedrock of social science. They are the principal means through which knowledge is advanced. Such articles provide content for textbooks, evidence for policy making, and fodder for legal, political, and pop-cultural debates.

There are currently thousands of journals that publish peer-reviewed research by social scientists. Journals with broad disciplinary purviews, such as the *American Journal of Psychology* and the *American Sociological Review*, have been joined by narrower (yet often interdisciplinary) outlets that focus on specialized topics, such as *Culture, Health, and Sexuality*, the *Journal of Early Childhood Literacy*, and the *Journal of Elder Abuse and Neglect*.

To neophytes, the world of journal science may seem foreign and complex. Many undergraduate and even some graduate students do not understand exactly how *journal articles* differ from the *articles* published in newspapers and magazines or from chapters published in books. The scholarly prose, extensive literature reviews, careful methodologies, and statistical tables may seem too daunting to penetrate. Indeed, many instructors shy away from assigning journal articles in class, favoring textbooks or readings from the popular press instead. Such instructors lack a brief guidebook that would make students less apprehensive (and more discerning) about social science articles.

This book demystifies the articles that are published in social science journals. In Chapter 1, I explain the basic premise of the book—the idea that social research is better than "common sense" but far from perfect—and give an overview of what's to come. In Chapter 2, I discuss how journal articles are written, reviewed, and published, drawing contrasts with other forms of academic and nonacademic scholarship. Then, in the body of the book, I elucidate seven key aspects of articles—conceptualization, literature reviews, measurement, sampling, analysis, ethics, and politics. In Chapters 3 through 9, I show how social scientists treat these issues with much more care and sophistication than laypersons generally do. Researchers exhibit much skill and determination; they deserve our respect and admiration. At the same time, social science should be read cautiously, if not skeptically. Thus, in each of these seven chapters, I highlight some of the recurring dilemmas and easy-to-spot imperfections that pervade much (if not all) of social research.

The main goal of the book is to encourage students to adopt a particular mind-set toward journal articles. This mind-set recognizes the many strengths of social research—especially its advantages over ordinary ways of knowing things. At the same time, this mind-set remains keenly aware that research is thoroughly and inevitably flawed. Rather than naïvely assuming that good research simply produces "The Truth," or cynically asserting that research is hopelessly biased and futile, I attempt to instill in readers a critical perspective—one that appreciates the strengths and the weaknesses of any piece of scholarship (cf. Best, 2001). After adopting this perspective, students should find journal articles less intimidating—and perhaps a lot more interesting. Chapter 10 provides some reasons why students should be personally motivated to read and use journal articles in their education, careers, and personal lives.

Exercises are included in Chapters 2 through 9. Readers can use these to practice or test out the book's ideas. Instructors may use the exercises as short graded assignments and as prompts for class discussion. Instructors who are somewhat ambitious may choose to combine these exercises into a longer term-paper assignment that requires students to analyze in detail a single article or a small collection of articles.

ACKNOWLEDGMENTS

I am grateful for the encouragement and advice I received from Jenine Harris and Vicki Knight. Also, thanks go to Joel Best for his mentorship—in person, over long distances, and through his scholarship. In addition, I would like to thank in advance the authors whose work I discuss in this book for their patience; my apologies if I overemphasize weaknesses or underappreciate strengths in your research.

I appreciate the thoughtful comments and suggestions provided by the reviewers:

Dr. Robert F. Abbey, Jr., *Troy University*
Osabuohien Amienyi, *Arkansas State University*
Joyce A. Arditti, *Virginia Tech*
Deborah Behan, *University of Texas at Arlington*
Kevin W. Borders, *Spalding University School of Social Work*
Alex J. Bowers, *The University of Texas at San Antonio*
April Idalski Carcone, *Wayne State University School of Medicine*
Brian L. Christenson, *Lewis-Clark State College*
Norma K. Clark, *Delaware State University*
Susan E. O. Field, *Georgian Court University*
Chad Morgan, *North Carolina Central University*

ABOUT THE AUTHOR

Scott R. Harris (PhD, University of Oregon) is Professor of Sociology at Saint Louis University, where he teaches courses on emotions, family, research methods, social psychology, and contemporary theory. He is the author of two books on conceptualization and measurement: *What Is Constructionism?* (for which received the Cooley Award from the Society for the Study of Symbolic Interaction) and *The Meanings of Marital Equality*. He also coedited *Making Sense of Social Problems* (with Joel Best) and coauthored *Stargazing: Celebrity, Fame, and Social Interaction* (with Kerry Ferris). He has reviewed articles for numerous journals and edited a special issue of the *Journal of Contemporary Ethnography*. Currently, he serves as Editor-in-Chief of the journal *Sociology Compass*.

CHAPTER 1

SOCIAL RESEARCH VERSUS ORDINARY WAYS OF KNOWING

As political comedians sometimes show, even the most "boring" news story can be made interesting—and possibly fun—depending on how you view it. Listening to the news can be valuable for the information one acquires, but it can be more edifying and entertaining to try to see through the apparently factual claims made by reporters, government officials, pundits, activists, and other commentators. By keeping in mind the idea that the truth is (almost) never exactly what someone claims it to be, news can be seen as a biased argument rather than an impartial description of reality. Somewhat similarly, it is possible to bring an irreverent attitude to social science journal articles. The standard article contains a lot of news but almost no entertainment value, at least on the surface. What's needed is for the reader to bring the right attitude to these scholarly works. A strong sense of irony—and the ability to ask the right questions—can help deflate even the most authoritative, statistic-laden, peer-reviewed publication.

How to Critique Journal Articles in the Social Sciences is not a jokebook, though. Its purpose is to help readers appreciate the rigor and complexity of social research while reducing the intimidation factor. When students understand in detail the inevitable frailty of most research, they are more likely to consider themselves worthy to enter into dialogue and debate with journal articles and even to attempt social research themselves. If this involves having a good laugh at authors' expense, so be it. (As long as we remember that our own claims may potentially be as problematic as others' claims, we're on relatively safe ground.)

After reading this book and practicing its exercises, any reasonably intelligent person should be able to challenge the wall of facts that social scientists so artfully manufacture and present. Out of the debris, however, we will always want to salvage some potentially valuable insights, perspectives, and statistics, imperfect though they may be. Research may be inescapably flawed, but it is still highly worthwhile.

So, right at the outset, let me be clear that I do hold social scientists in high regard, and I hope that—after reading this book—you will as well. Any author whose work I criticize can also be complimented for exhibiting a great deal of skill and determination.

One way to convey the respect I have for social scientists—and to encourage readers to feel the same—is to compare social research to some of the alternative ways of knowing that can be found in everyday life.

☆ ORDINARY HUMAN INQUIRY

There are many ways of generating and validating information about the world. First, people can simply use their "common sense" and apply their society's conventional wisdom to a situation. Or, a person may simply turn to an authority figure for the truth—such as a parent, teacher, politician, or radio talk show host. Those who are religious may consult sacred texts for truths about the world, pray for insight, or consult an oracle. People read newspapers, magazines, and websites; watch television; exchange informational e-mails; and discuss current affairs with their friends. If they hear advice about a self-improvement strategy—perhaps for dieting, getting better grades, or maintaining close relationships—individuals may test out the idea via informal attempts at trial and error.

For the sake of simplicity, I would like to lump all these sorts of practices together and call them *ordinary human inquiry* or *everyday ways of knowing* (see Babbie, 2010). This loose category can then be contrasted with *social research,* the more germane topic for this book. Crudely put, there are nonscientific ways of knowing and there are scientific ways of knowing. As their name suggests, social scientists try to pursue the latter—to the degree they can—and they should be recognized and commended for their efforts.

☆ SIX DIFFERENCES BETWEEN ORDINARY HUMAN INQUIRY AND SOCIAL SCIENCE

When confronted with an issue they want to learn about, social scientists go to great lengths to study the topic as carefully and rigorously as feasible. Their efforts far exceed the attempts that laypersons make in everyday life. In this section, I will outline six ways that social researchers go well beyond ordinary ways of knowing. These differences parallel the structure of journal articles, and foreshadow the main topics covered in this book.

Conceptualizing the Topic

First, researchers carefully conceptualize their research questions. Scholars try to formulate precisely what topic they are studying and what they want to know about it. For example, a researcher may be interested in *the causes of poverty* but is unlikely to be content with that phrase. A journal article on this topic would likely specify what *poverty* means and would distinguish different kinds of causes (such as structural vs. individual; economic factors at the global, national, and local levels, etc.). Scholars want to carefully delineate that which they are studying and that which they are not.

Compare this with ordinary human inquiry, where two friends (or news pundits, etc.) may engage in a heated discussion without spending much time specifying the question at hand: What is their conversation about? What specific issue are they trying to address? Conversations often ramble from topic to topic with little attention given to setting the parameters of the debate. Terms may be used extremely loosely, and few people stop to compare their definitions to make sure they are talking about the same thing.

As we'll see in Chapter 3, social researchers usually do better than laypersons at conceptualizing the issues they want to address. Nevertheless, research is far from perfect. Key terms may be relatively carefully defined, but these definitions contain ambiguities that can't be fully eliminated. And, different researchers propose divergent definitions of the same concept, leading to contradictions and confusion when readers move from article to article.

Reading the Literature: Quantity and Quality

A second key difference between ordinary human inquiry and social science is the reading that is involved. In everyday life, it is common for people to express confident opinions on a meager basis. Our seemingly well-informed companions may skim the *New York Times*, FoxNews.com, or nothing at all. They may pontificate enthusiastically after listening to a radio talk show or watching a local news broadcast.

Social scientists, in contrast, read prolifically. (When friends or relatives ask me to comment on a social issue, I sometimes say that I would prefer to read several scholarly publications before I formulate an opinion.) And it's not just the quantity—the quality of what scholars read matters just as much. Social scientists read rigorous, peer-reviewed publications written by authors who have devoted years or decades to becoming experts on a given topic. Whereas popular news coverage can almost always be skimmed quickly, scholarly work can at times require a slow, painstaking process of reading and rereading. Perhaps because reality is complex, scholars' work is equally complex. Readers must carefully navigate dense paragraphs and technical terms while underlining key passages, commenting in the margins, and giving due attention to crucial details revealed in tiny footnotes.

Obtaining a Ph.D. requires a tremendous amount of reading in order to become familiar with the current state of the literature in one's disciplinary subfield. Then, social scientists must continue to read throughout their careers if their own research projects are to make contributions to the constantly evolving debates that occur on the pages of scholarly journals.

However, as well-read as scholars may be, they cannot read everything. No one can claim to keep abreast of the (literally) thousands of journal articles that are published each year—not to mention books—that might contain some theory, method, or finding that is relevant to his or her work. Even narrowly circumscribed subfields can advance at a rapid pace. Moreover, any single article can be "read" or interpreted in different ways, and a careful reading does not guarantee your interpretation is correct. Just as different people have different reactions to movies or to religious scriptures, different scholars can draw divergent implications from a particular article or group of articles. As I will show in Chapter 4, a seemingly objective literature review inevitably involves some arbitrary, selective, and interpretive decision making about what to read and what sense to make of it.

Taking Careful Measurements

In everyday life, people loosely measure the phenomena they are interested in, such as "good" versus "bad" television shows or "fair" versus "unfair" behavior by friends and coworkers. Often, these "measurements" are merely haphazard impressions and hazy memories. Social scientists, in contrast, attempt to develop standardized measurement procedures that can be consciously and systematically applied to a wide range of occurrences of a particular phenomenon. This is called *operationalization*. It allows scholars to be more explicit, thorough, and evenhanded as they collect examples and evidence.

For example, people may casually determine how hardworking or lazy a college student is. "You always seem to be partying," or "You never have any fun," friends or relatives may say. Such claims might be based on a few informal conversations or casual observations. Imagine a more scientific approach. To determine how hardworking a student is, one might want to specify different kinds of labor—such as schoolwork, paid employment, volunteering, and family obligations. Then, one might want to develop a system for asking—such as a carefully constructed questionnaire—exactly how many hours per week a student tends to spend on each activity. Data could also be collected regarding the number of hours the student spends on leisure so that comparisons could be made between time devoted to working and nonworking activities.

Chapter 5 will explain why social scientists' measurements are better than laypersons' but still far from perfect. Researchers may present their measurement strategies as obvious or straightforward, but they usually involve subjective choices. (For example, should some family obligations count as work or leisure or both?) There are usually many different ways to measure a variable. Different scholars make different choices, which shape the results of their research. The problem of inter-researcher discontinuity casts doubt on whether different studies of the "same" topic are comparable and cumulative.

Collecting Samples

Imagine you want to decide whether to take a course with Professor Smith. Of course, all professors are geniuses who excel at nearly everything. Yet, for some reason, you want to know, in advance, whether Prof. Smith is a good teacher. You might be tempted to ask a couple friends who took a course from Smith. Or, you might find a dozen evaluations of Smith on a public website similar to www.ratemyprofessors.com. You might be tempted to treat these inquiries as sufficient. No offense—social scientists would not.

Assuming Prof. Smith teaches more than 100 students every year, the two friends are a pretty small sample on which to generalize about a person's teaching ability. The (often small) number of evaluations on www .ratemyprofessors.com may also be problematic, especially if the students who use the website tend to do so when they have negative feelings about their instructors or when they are principally concerned with "easy grading." In addition, the website's ratings may have been posted over a period of years, producing a sample of, say, 20 individuals out of several hundred. And since the website isn't policed very well, the same student may submit several evaluations while pretending to be a different person each time.

In everyday life, people are free to draw inferences—and jump to conclusions—based on weak, haphazardly collected samples. Researchers try to do better.

Researchers tend to collect samples that are much larger and more carefully assembled than those collected by laypersons. Sometimes an entire population can be studied—similar to when an instructor collects teaching evaluations from all of the students enrolled in a course. Usually, though, researchers gather a sample of the relevant data. While doing this, they pay attention to exactly how their sample is selected, who or what makes it into the sample, and the degree to which generalizing is warranted. Researchers tend to use better procedures, collect better samples, and extrapolate more cautiously.

Still, virtually no sampling system is perfect. Scholars have limited time and resources. Their selection procedures involve trade-offs and judgment calls and produce samples with regrettable deficiencies and drawbacks. Then, scholars sometimes generalize too far from their samples and make unwarranted assertions about larger populations. Chapter 6 will discuss how to identify both the strengths and the weaknesses of authors' strategies for sampling and generalizing.

Analyzing Data and Presenting Results

So far I've suggested that laypersons tend to jump from topic to topic without clearly defining the issue at hand or the key terms they're using to discuss it; they take very loose measurements (if any) of the phenomena involved; and they overgeneralize from small, haphazardly collected samples. A related but distinguishable tendency is the manner in which people analyze and present any "data" that they actually possess.

Laypersons often make exaggerated claims about causal connections, sometimes using absolutist adjectives such as *always* and *never.* For example, a husband might tell his wife, "You're always complaining about your coworkers. You have a bad attitude." Or, a wife might tell her husband, "You're completely self-centered. You never do the dishes." Usually, these kinds of statements are based on weak measurement and data collection, as we've already discussed; moreover, these statements tend to involve hasty analyses and inaccurate descriptions of the data being discussed.

Social scientists do not need to make snap judgments in the course of a heated conversation. Instead, during the months or years they devote to writing their journal articles, they can calmly take their time and systematically crunch the numbers. Researchers can use statistical software to process hundreds or thousands of pieces of data about a wide range of causal factors and events in order to determine whether certain variables are correlated with each other. For example, researchers might collect questionnaires from several thousand high school students in order to determine whether marijuana smoking tends to be associated with delinquency or if other variables are superior predictors. Researchers tend not to present their findings in terms of simple yes or no, but provide qualifying details about the precise degree to which variables may be related, and they highlight weaknesses in their work that limit its potential accuracy. To use some fancy lingo, scholars usually prefer circumspection and precision to melodrama.

Nevertheless, even the most rigorous data analysis involves subjective choices. Social scientists can never analyze all the variables that are relevant to a study; they must choose a small number of issues to focus on. In addition, it is often difficult for scholars to determine the causal order of their independent and dependent variables—a version of the dilemma "Which came first—the chicken or the egg?" For instance, does drug use tend to lead to delinquency, or does a pattern of delinquency usually come first?

The kinds of data analyses that appear in journal articles are often overwhelmingly technical. The mathematical equations and tables can generate awe, fear, or dread. Any newcomer may wonder, "Who am I to question such statistical geniuses?" By the end of Chapter 7, you'll see that even a social science newbie can identify strengths and weaknesses in the most technical article.

Ethics and Politics

In everyday life, people regularly avoid sensitive, politically charged topics. Many families avoid religion and politics at the dinner table. Coworkers might frown upon someone who raises the topic of same-sex marriage at the water cooler. "Stick to sports, television shows, and celebrity gossip—those are safer topics," we tell ourselves and our companions.

Yet, at the same time, people don't seem to realize that even "safe" inquiries can be fraught with peril. A simple question—such as "Why didn't you go to Prof. Smith's class yesterday?"—might be more risky than we realize. Perhaps a student was absent due to a problem with drugs or alcohol, a death in the family, or an emotional breakdown due to being dumped by a boyfriend or girlfriend. And then, once people learn sensitive information about a friend or acquaintance, there is a tendency to share it with others via "secrets" (a.k.a. gossip) that can spread quickly and damage personal reputations.

In comparison, social scientists try to be more cautious about what they ask, whom they reveal personal information to, and what the effects of their inquiries might be. Researchers certainly do not shy away from sensitive, politically charged topics. Yet, whether they are asking about someone's age, education level, self-esteem, sexual experiences, or religious beliefs, researchers carefully think about what they will ask and what they will do with the information.

Researchers follow the codes of ethics established by the scholarly associations they belong to; they submit their research proposals to their universities' Institutional Review Boards for careful examination and approval before collecting data; and they read what prior scholars have written about the ethics of research. Scholars think about how best to phrase questions and how to store personal information so it can't be accidentally viewed or purposefully stolen. When writing their articles, researchers take steps to disguise the identities of their respondents so that readers cannot link discrediting information to any particular individuals.

Still, ethics and politics are interpretive matters, involving subjective standards and viewpoints. There is usually more than one way to answer questions like "What's the right (ethical) thing to do here?" and "What good (political) goal might this study help accomplish?" In Chapter 8, we'll explore some strategies for identifying the dilemmas and trade-offs in researchers' ethical choices. In Chapter 9, we'll discuss ways of challenging authors' politics.

☆ CONCLUSION

As you can see, there is a recurring theme that runs through this book: Research is better than ordinary human inquiry but is far from perfect. Chapters 3 through 9 apply this theme to the most important aspects of social research: conceptualization, literature reviews, measurement, sampling, analysis, ethics, and politics. Chapter 10 offers some reasons for reading journal articles despite their flaws.

After finishing this book, you should be able to appreciate the strengths of research without being overwhelmed by it, and you should be able to identify the weaknesses of research without rejecting it entirely. Ideally, this book will encourage you to approach journal articles with a mind-set that is neither naïve nor cynical. I hope you will pursue the middle path—be a critical consumer of the information and insights that social science can offer you (Best, 2001).

CHAPTER 2

WHAT IS A JOURNAL ARTICLE?

Like most words, the term *article* can have multiple meanings depending on the context. People outside of academia may think of newspapers and popular magazines when they hear the word *article*. Similarly, the idea of a journal may conjure up images of a diary or personal log of some sort.[1] These connotations perturb researchers. It is no small feat to publish an article in a peer-reviewed academic journal. Such articles differ significantly from what appears in a local newspaper (such as the *St. Louis Post-Dispatch* or the *Los Angeles Times*), although that kind of writing can be important too. Informative articles also appear in periodicals such as *Rolling Stone*, *Sports Illustrated*, *Time,* or *Newsweek,* or on websites like CNN.com or the HuffingtonPost.com. But academic journals differ in several significant respects from these sorts of popular outlets. I'll explain seven differences below.

JOURNAL ARTICLES VERSUS ARTICLES PUBLISHED IN POPULAR OUTLETS ☆

1) Journal articles are usually lengthier than popular articles.

Articles in the popular press often (but not always) contain only a few paragraphs or pages of text. In contrast, social science journal articles are much longer. The average article probably runs 25 double-spaced pages in length when printed from a personal computer (or around 6,000 words).

---

[1] Indeed, some neophyte undergraduates mistakenly use the word *stories* (without any postmodern irony) to refer to journal articles, as in "That was a good story we read for class today."

Article length varies by outlet, though. The *American Sociological Review (ASR)* limits authors to a total of 15,000 words; the *American Journal of Public Health (AJPH)* sets the maximum at 3,500 words.[2]

2) Journal articles take more time to compose.

Although there are exceptions, newspaper or magazine articles may be written in less than a week or even less than a day. Journalists should be applauded for their efforts to understand and convey the latest happenings while meeting frenetic deadlines. However, scholarly researchers should be applauded for their efforts too. My guess is that the average journal article takes six months to complete—six months of part- or full-time labor. Some may be written in a matter of weeks; others take a year or more.

3) Journal articles involve extensive reviews of the literature.

In the process of preparing to write an article, a scholar may read dozens if not hundreds of relevant works. The author may cite only a fraction of these and include them in the reference section, but there are likely many other texts they have read before and during the time they spent composing their own work. Scholars must almost always carefully indicate how their own work builds on or compares to previously published work. Usually, authors of newspaper and magazine articles are under no such obligation, though they may occasionally mention a recent publication or interview an expert.

4) Journal articles typically involve more rigorous exploration of theoretical assumptions.

Scholars spend much time thinking and writing about the theoretical frameworks that they operate within. Any piece of data, or any set of facts, can be interpreted in different ways. One reason why academic authors conduct extensive literature reviews is so they can carefully consider the various theoretical perspectives that may be brought to bear on their topics. Authors may then make informed but creative use of these perspectives, for example, by attempting to contrast or integrate Marxism with particular ideas from functionalism, symbolic interactionism, feminism, or rational choice theory.

---

[2] Downloaded November 12, 2012, from http://www.sagepub.com/journalsProdDesc.nav?ct_ p=manuscriptSubmission&prodId=Journal201969&currTree=Subjects&level1=N00 and http:// ajph.aphapublications.org/userimages/ContentEditor/1318438422261/Instructions_for_Authors .pdf. AJPH maximum does not include references;, the ASR maximum does.

5) Academic journals are usually competitive, and the editors accept a minority of submissions.

Better academic journals—such as *Social Problems* and the *Journal of Personality and Social Psychology*—tend to accept only 10% to 15% of the articles that are submitted. Less prestigious outlets may average a 20% to 50% acceptance rate. This differs from the kinds of newspaper or magazine articles that editors may assign to a journalist on their staff, with the expectation that a reasonably well-written piece has a high likelihood of appearing later that day, week, or month. Publishing an academic article involves a higher risk of rejection as experts compete against each other for coveted journal space. It's a grueling process that can last months or years in part because of the next point.

6) Academic journal articles are evaluated by an anonymous panel of experts before being accepted for publication.

After an author spends an average of six months writing an article, he or she is still many months if not years away from seeing the work in print. This is in large part due to the screening process that journals use. Journal editors rely on a large cadre of volunteer peer reviewers to evaluate submitted manuscripts. Except for manuscripts that an editor rejects out of hand (e.g., due to low quality or inappropriate topic), journal articles are subjected to harsh scrutiny from experts who may have (in many cases) already published on the article's general topic. Usually, the review process is double-blind: The peer reviewers do not know who the author is and vice versa. This allows reviewers to be frank and forthcoming in their criticisms. Editors obtain feedback from about three reviewers, examine the reviewers' comments, and send a decision letter to the article's author. This stage of the process usually takes a few months, and the outcome is almost never an immediate acceptance. In most cases, the outcome is rejection. The remaining authors are invited to revise and resubmit their manuscripts after composing a new draft that takes into account the criticisms of reviewers. Making those changes can take days, weeks, or months, then the author's revised draft may (depending on the editor's discretion) be subjected to yet another round of peer review.

Newspaper and magazine articles may be put through various editorial screening processes, but rarely are they as rigorously vetted as journal articles.

7) Journal articles often report the results of authors' original research using empirical data that is collected via careful methodological strategies.

Scholars tend to spend a lot of time thinking about their samples, interview questions, data analysis techniques, and so on. Researchers aren't perfect, but they usually do much more than quote eye witnesses or government officials. Social scientists try to do something resembling science, which—after taking a course or two on methodology—any undergraduate should be able to recognize as distinct from much (but not all) of what journalists do.

☆ JOURNAL ARTICLES VERSUS CHAPTERS IN BOOKS

To an untrained eye, the articles that appear in an issue of a journal may look like chapters that appear in a book. A single issue of a journal may contain as many as 10 or 15 articles and run well over 100 pages in length. To an inexperienced reader, an issue of an academic journal may look like a book of some sort. Moreover, when libraries collect a year's worth of issues and bind them together, the result is something that may look like a very long and impressive tome.

Yet, there are some important differences between journal articles and book chapters.

1) Compared to the articles that appear in an issue of a journal, the chapters of a book are usually more closely related to each other, often flowing in a linear or cumulative fashion.

Whether authored by a sole individual or assembled by an editor who gathers the works of others, book chapters tend to lead from one into the other and then add up to some larger whole that hangs together. In contrast, journals often include articles that (comparatively) have little to do with each other. In the vast majority of cases, the authors of adjoined papers did not know they were each contributing to the same issue. Journal editors usually do not solicit the papers as part of a preplanned, coherent theme. And each paper tends to be crafted as a stand-alone piece—as a paper that does not depend on or in any way refer to the other articles that appear in the same issue.

Metaphorically speaking, the articles that appear in a journal are more like hotel guests who coincidentally reserved a room on the same floor rather than close friends or family members who purposefully share a house together.

There are some exceptions to this tendency, the foremost being special issues. An issue of a journal is special not because it is intellectually challenged in some way (though skeptical readers may occasionally have doubts) but because its papers were solicited, reviewed, and assembled in light of a particular theme.[3]

2) Chapters in edited books are more frequently invited submissions rather than open submissions.

When a scholar gets an idea (and interest from a publisher) to edit a book on a particular topic, she or he will contact prospective authors who have expertise related to a subtheme of that topic. The editor informs authors of her or his plans to edit a book, including its overall theme and its potential sections and chapters. Contributors accept or decline invitations depending on whether they like the sound of the project, whether they think they can meet the editor's proposed deadline, and other factors.

With journals, usually none of this takes place. Journals accept submissions year-round, with virtually no holidays or breaks, from the moment they are founded to the moment they become defunct. (Some journals live for many decades or over a century; others die in their youth or middle age.) Authors do not need a personal invitation to contribute a paper to a journal. Virtually anybody can submit an article at any time on any topic, and the journal editor will be obligated to at least skim it to determine whether its quality and content merit peer review. (Go ahead—submit a class paper and see what happens! Or, just take my word for it, and leave those busy editors alone.)

3) Book chapters are less likely to undergo the same rigorous peer-review process that journal articles do.

It is usually easier to publish a book chapter than a journal article in a top journal. There are exceptions—some edited books are rigorously screened and evaluated by anonymous experts. (And even when a chapter is not rigorously reviewed, that doesn't necessarily mean it is no good.) But book chapters may be evaluated only (or primarily) by the book's editor rather than by a team of anonymous experts. Now put yourself in the editor's place. What would be more difficult: rejecting an unsolicited manuscript for a journal that has an ongoing, rolling submission process or rejecting an

---

[3] Special issues are produced differently: A call for papers is announced in the journal and other strategic locations; potential authors consider whether it is feasible or desirable for them to contribute a paper (perhaps a work-in-progress or a new project) by the stated deadline; the editor arranges for peer reviews of submitted works with an eye toward assembling an appropriately sized collection (perhaps four to eight papers, depending on the journal) that addresses the issue theme and hangs together in some way.

invited manuscript for a book that has a deadline for completion? Authors are less likely to receive a rejection letter if they were personally asked to make contributions and if their papers are needed to complete a finite and time-sensitive book project.

This, of course, doesn't mean book chapters aren't valuable. They can sometimes offer authors more flexibility to make innovative contributions to their fields or present opportunities to write in accessible language that is useful for classroom instruction. Chapters should not be dismissed, but it should be recognized that journal articles are usually more rigorously reviewed.

☆ WHERE CAN SCHOLARLY ARTICLES BE FOUND? THE DIVERSE LANDSCAPE OF ACADEMIC JOURNALS

So far, I have suggested that journal articles are different from and more rigorous than the works that appear in popular outlets and even the chapters that appear in scholarly books. Now that we've made these distinctions and comparisons, let's look at the outlets in which social science articles do tend to appear.

There are literally thousands of social science journals currently in operation in the world. Probably dozens are born or die with each passing year. The database *Sociological Abstracts*—one of many electronic resources useful for locating journal articles—monitors more than 1,800 serials for content relevant to sociology.[4] The database *PsycINFO* includes content from almost 2,500 journals related to psychology, and *Education Abstracts* indexes articles from 680 journals related to education.[5] Keep in mind that the content of these three databases partially overlaps as some journals address multiple audiences.

One way to map out the landscape of academic journals is to make a tentative distinction between disciplinary and interdisciplinary outlets. There are, of course, many journals devoted specifically to a particular social science discipline, such as *Sociological Quarterly* or the *American Journal of Psychology*. However, the boundaries between disciplines are somewhat permeable and increasingly so. There are now many interdisciplinary journals—such as *Social Science and Medicine* or the *Journal of*

---

[4] Downloaded on November 12, 2012, from
http://www.csa.com/factsheets/socioabs-set-c.php

[5] Downloaded November 12, 2012, from
http://www.apa.org/pubs/databases/psycinfo/index.aspx and
http://www.ebscohost.com/academic/education-abstracts

Family Issues—that publish work by scholars from a wide range of backgrounds and expertise.

It can take some investigation to recognize the scholarly home of some journals. For instance, *Social Psychology Quarterly* is (for the most part) produced by and for sociologists; the *Journal of Social Issues* caters (primarily) to psychologists. Some journals specialize in somewhat narrower subfields or topics, but they can still be either disciplinary or interdisciplinary. For example, many disciplines might have something important to say about the topic of *Motivation and Emotion*, but the editorial board, authorship, and readers of that journal seems to be primarily psychologists.

As I mentioned earlier in this chapter, some academic journals have better reputations than others. An article published in a top journal such as the *American Sociological Review* will likely be seen differently than an article that appears in a still-respected but easier-to-get-accepted journal such as *Sociological Forum*. The more competitive the outlet, the more strenuous the review process, which lends credibility and visibility to a piece of research.[6]

Undergraduate and graduate students should beware: Your instructors will judge your work in part based on the types of sources you cite in your papers. A serious student tends to cite journals rather than websites or newspapers, and outstanding students have a better awareness of what journals their professors will deem most prestigious and appropriate in their disciplines. This is no easy matter as, occasionally, an instructor will have a low opinion of a top journal while giving great respect to a lesser-known journal that better fits his or her methodological or theoretical preferences. And, keep in mind that second- or third-tier journals are still useful and sometimes publish papers that are easier to read and understand.

WHAT GETS PUBLISHED IN ACADEMIC JOURNALS? OTHER SCHOLARLY WORKS BESIDES EMPIRICAL RESEARCH ARTICLES ☆

If you are a serious student in the social sciences, eventually you will need to "graduate" from the realm of websites, newspapers, and magazines—and even from textbooks and book chapters. You'll need to enter the complex world of academic journals. It is there that you will find articles that report original analyses of data—those *empirical* studies that are the focus of this book.

---

[6]Along with acceptance and rejection rates, scholars sometimes use impact factors to evaluate that scholars sometimes use to evaluate the prestige of a journal. *Impact factors* are measures that capture the average number of times a paper is cited by other scholars. Prestigious journals tend to publish papers that are more widely read and cited.

To successfully locate empirical articles, there is another dimension of diversity you'll need to consider. Not only is there diversity among journals—such as disciplinary versus interdisciplinary outlets—there are many different categories of work published within journals.

Below I'll describe five kinds of publications that are not conventional research articles but which may appear side-by-side with them on the pages of academic journals.

1) Book reviews and review essays

Some journals publish short reviews (usually one to two pages) of recently published books. Less frequently a review essay will be published; in these, a reviewer uses several pages of space to discuss and evaluate a few recently published books that all focus on the same topic. Book reviews and review essays always seem to appear in the back pages of the journal rather than in the front—probably a sign of their comparatively lower status compared to standard journal articles. An exception would be those few journals that specialize only in publishing book reviews and review essays, such as *Contemporary Sociology* and *Contemporary Psychology*.

2) Theoretical treatises

Sometimes journals publish papers that make arguments about theoretical perspectives or sets of perspectives without systematically collecting and analyzing data. Authors may reexamine a great thinkers' key texts or propose new integrations or innovations of seemingly disparate sources in order to derive insights that can be applied to particular topics or subfields. Theoretical treatises may use real-life examples to illustrate ideas, but they are still different from empirical journal articles.

3) Literature reviews

Closely related to theoretical treatises are papers that attempt to summarize (and make arguments about) previous publications on a topic. What do we know about topic X? What are the strengths and weaknesses of current research on Y? In which direction should scholars who study Z go next? Journals sometimes publish these papers right alongside empirical studies. Alternatively, these papers can be found in specialty journals that only publish lit review articles, such as the prestigious Annual Review series (e.g., *Annual Review of Psychology*,

Annual Review of Public Health) or the helpful Compass series (e.g., *Geography Compass, Sociology Compass*).[7]

4) Methodological pieces

Also published in journals are papers that discuss, develop, or evaluate specific methodological practices or techniques. These pieces may look a lot like conventional research, but their main focus is on improving the methodological procedures that authors can use in subsequent research rather than on reporting new findings derived from data collection and analysis.

5) Notes, commentaries, and responses

Journals sometimes publish a "Note From the Editor" at the beginning, where an editor expounds upon his or her vision for the journal in general or gives an interpretation or introduction to the articles that appear in a particular issue. Perhaps confusingly, there are also "Research Notes" and "Research Briefs." These types of notes are sometimes simply shorter versions of research articles or discussions of preliminary or tentative findings. *Commentaries,* in turn, can be seen as (usually) highly intelligent letters that readers or reviewers submit about an article that appeared in the journal. *Responses* are how authors react to those letters. Sometimes, these commentaries and responses appear in the same issue as the article that provoked the conversation, as editors can arrange for these exchanges to take place during the months before an article appears in print. Other times, commentaries and responses may be published months or years after a provocative article first appears in print.

AND FINALLY, WHAT DO CONVENTIONAL ARTICLES LOOK LIKE? THE TYPICAL FORMAT OF THE STANDARD JOURNAL ARTICLE ☆

In this book, we will be concerned primarily with articles that report the findings of empirical social research. These papers are the lifeblood of social science in that their purpose is to advance knowledge by collecting evidence and testing theories. Empirical articles are the main reason that most social science journals exist.

---

[7]Another type of journal publication, called *meta-analysis,* occupies the border between standard empirical articles and literature reviews. In meta-analyses, scholars use statistical methods to combine the findings of previous research conducted by various authors and reported in many different articles.

Like snowflakes, no two journal articles are identical. However (and also like snowflakes), most research articles do tend to look pretty similar when viewed from a distance. For the remainder of this chapter, let's use the acronym SJA to refer to standard journal articles, meaning publications that report the findings of empirical social science research. Most SJAs follow a fairly predictable format and contain similar elements.

1) Title and abstract

An SJA includes an easy-to-spot title near the top of the first page of text. Underneath is almost always an *abstract*,[8] or summary of the article that was written by the authors, not by the editor of the journal. Most abstracts consist of one paragraph typed in italics. Some journals, however, require authors to compose abstracts that contain four concise parts, separated by headings such as "Background," "Methods," "Results," and "Conclusion." Authors are usually limited to a tight word-length, usually 100 words but sometimes as many as 250 words.[9]

2) Introduction and literature review

An SJA begins with a statement of the problem and a review of the literature that has been written on the topic. Scholars attempt to justify the significance of the topic and explain the contribution they intend their paper to make. For example, an article on the causes of poverty might begin by discussing pervious research on the prevalence of poverty and its association with harmful social problems. Then, certain gaps or weaknesses in the literature may be highlighted, and the research at hand will be framed as an attempt to overcome those limitations. Arriving at a new-and-improved understanding of poverty (or whatever topic) could improve the state of society and the discipline at the same time— that sort of formula makes for a powerful introduction.

3) Methods section

Following the title, abstract, introduction, and literature review, SJAs typically describe the strategies that the researchers used to collect, measure, and analyze their data. To continue with our previous example, researchers

---

[8] In some contexts the word *abstract* is used to criticize a statement for being too vague or theoretical, but that is not the meaning of the term here, where it is even pronounced differently—with an emphasis on the first syllable rather than the second.

[9] A minor element of SJAs to mention is the journal information—the name and the volume, issue, and page numbers of the journal in which the article appears, along with the date. A basic but good place to start in evaluating an SJA is to notice this information at the top or bottom of the first page.

studying poverty might explain how they selected a group of people, places, or information to include in their study; how they operationalized (measured) income, race, health, education, and other variables; and what statistical software programs and analytical techniques they used to look for causal relationships between those variables.

4) Findings

SJAs typically proceed next to a section that presents their "Findings," which also could be labeled "Analysis," "Results," or something similar. In quantitative articles, authors may elaborate further on the techniques used to analyze the data, but they will spend the majority of this section of the paper summarizing the results via a series of tables that often contain percentages, equations, coefficients, p-values, and other mathematical terminology (which you don't need to understand for the purposes of this book). Qualitative articles will likely present data in the form of quotes— for example, excerpts from interviews or from the researchers' field notes. (This characterization of quantitative and qualitative articles is exceedingly brief; there are many complicated varieties of and overlaps between the two.)

5) Discussion and conclusion

Another major aspect of SJAs is the discussion and conclusion, which could appear in a single section or in separate sections. Here, authors attempt to highlight the important findings obtained via their research so that readers don't miss them. Authors also draw connections to their earlier literature review—for example, by arguing that their work has contradicted or confirmed previous research or pushed the field forward in some way. SJAs sometimes contain a discussion of the implications that their work has for policy making or practical action of some sort as well as a mention of the study's weaknesses that future research should keep in mind and attempt to overcome.

6) Endnotes and footnotes

Not all journals allow either endnotes or footnotes—the sentences that appear (usually) in smaller font after the last paragraph of text or at the bottom of each page—but many do. Scholars use these notes to address a range of issues that might otherwise disrupt the flow of their prose: They acknowledge and respond to a criticism that a peer reviewer made on a particular passage; they cite a previous publication that has some relevance (such as confirmatory or contradictory ideas), and so on. Footnotes and endnotes can be easy for nonacademics to overlook, but serious scholars know that the "the devil is in the details," and some of the most interesting details can be found in that tiny print.

7) References

The last section of an SJA contains the books, articles, and other sources that the authors cited in their article. These are usually listed alphabetically but can be numbered in a manner similar to footnotes or endnotes. Nonacademics might presume that reference sections contain everything that authors read on a subject before they conducted their research. This would be far off the mark, as authors usually have read widely and only cite a fraction of that material in their published works.

☆ CONCLUSION

In this book, we will focus on most but not all of these seven elements of SJAs. I see little point in critiquing titles and abstracts, for example. My goal is to provide readers with ideas and strategies for *actively engaging*—critically examining and challenging—the claims to accuracy, comprehensiveness, and objectivity that authors explicitly or implicitly make in SJAs. Therefore, my emphasis will be on what seem to be the main components of standard articles: the introduction and literature review, the methods section, the analysis of data and presentation of results, and the discussion and conclusion.

I defined SJAs generally as "papers reporting empirical research," but this book will more specifically emphasize *quantitative* articles—those that employ statistical analysis. I do this for several reasons. Compared to qualitative research, quantitative research tends to be published in the top journals more often, receive grant funding more often, and be perceived as more objective or scientific. Quantitative research is more intimidating, as the details of the analytical techniques are usually beyond the comprehension of anyone who has not taken courses in statistics.

After reading this book, I want students to be able to (1) appreciate the strengths of research compared to ordinary human inquiry and (2) identify the inevitable weaknesses of research. Quantitative research is much more fear- and awe-inspiring than qualitative research. If I can give students the skills and confidence to read and critique quantitative research, then the odds are good they will be able to do the same for qualitative research. So, my main (but not exclusive) emphasis will be on the former more than the latter kind of research.

EXERCISE 2.1.

Here are two simple exercises to ensure you have some direct exposure to the world of journal articles. Journals exist both in print and online, so let's look at both venues.

1. **Locate the print version of at least one social science journal in your field.** By *locate*, I mean look up the name of the journal in the catalog of your university's library, go to the correct floor, and find the bound copies of the journal on the shelves. I recommend you choose an older, well-established journal—perhaps something with the name *American Journal of "X"* (where X = Anthropology, Education, Political Science, Psychology, Sociology, etc.)—but your instructor and librarian can offer suggestions as well.

   • Skim through an entire year of the journal; usually, each year of the journal is bound together in a single hard-back volume. Notice the range of topics, the seriousness of the prose, and the technical sophistication of the analyses. Pick one article that interests you, and copy the title page or the entire article if you prefer. Report back to your instructor the reasons why that article caught your attention.

   • How many feet of shelf space does the journal occupy in your library? Loosely measure that, and report back to your instructor.

   The goal is for you to develop an appreciation for the history, scope, and size of journals—and the fun that can be had when you stumble across an interesting paper merely by skimming through the stacks.

2. **Locate the website for at least one social science journal in your field.** By *locate*, I mean Google the name of the journal, perhaps putting it in quotes, until you find the correct site. You can use the same journal as you did in #1 or a different journal.

   • Skim through the tables of contents for several recent issues of the journal. Do you notice any pros or cons of searching electronically verses searching in the library?

   • Locate the webpage titled "Submission Guidelines" or "Instructions for Authors" and skim through it. Print the first page of the screen or copy and paste the contents into a Word doc and print the first page of that. Tell your instructor about any guidelines that you find interesting or confusing.

CHAPTER 3

DEFINING KEY TERMS

On any given day, you're likely to have dozens of conversations with friends, relatives, coworkers, and acquaintances. The topics may at times be trivial—such as good movies or what happened at the party last night—but nevertheless you're always talking about something. Even the most casual conversation has at least one topic of concern.

But what exactly are the things that we discuss and debate in our daily lives? Can we define what we are talking about?

This straightforward question can, surprisingly, be very difficult to answer. If a friend were to ask for clarification—as in "So what exactly are your criteria for a *good movie*?" or "What specifically differentiates a *party* from other kinds of gatherings?"—it is doubtful that you would have a ready-made, clear-cut list of ideas to offer. We would likely give answers that were spontaneous and vague or else avoid the question entirely, treating the inquiry as odd.

In journal articles, social scientists do a better job of defining their key terms than ordinary conversationalists do. Scholars take more time to formulate and explain the concepts they use in their research. Research involves technical language, and it is important that readers comprehend what authors are trying to convey.

Nevertheless, even the most intelligent scholar cannot achieve complete clarity and precision. How can this be? That's what this chapter will show you. By the end, you should be able to critique virtually any article you encounter by highlighting its unstated and inevitable ambiguities.

Lest you mistake this chapter for a mean-spirited attack on social research, let's remember the theme of this book: Research is better than ordinary human inquiry and is useful, but it's far from perfect. Hence, we'll start this chapter by thinking a bit more about conceptualization in everyday life.

That will help us keep things in proper perspective and appreciate the positive habits and skills that social scientists exhibit before we focus on the conceptual flaws that haunt journal articles.

☆ DEFINING CONCEPTS IN EVERYDAY LIFE

Consider a practice that is familiar to many college students: drinking alcohol. Not everyone drinks, and some ingest alcohol only sporadically and in small doses. Others, of course, drink frequently and in large quantities. Their drinking does not escape notice—perhaps because of the behaviors that accompany inebriation—and so we become interested in and talk about these people. How should we describe them?

We have many choices. For example, I have heard some drinkers portrayed as *boozers, fish, lushes, heavy drinkers,* and *hard-core partiers.* These terms are, arguably, highly vague. I have heard them used confidently but never defined explicitly. We might invoke such terms in order to praise someone ("John, you drink like a *fish*—I wish I had your stamina"), to criticize a person ("Mary *drinks heavily,* and that's just not my idea of a good time"), or to move a conversation in a serious or humorous direction ("Wayne is a total *lush*—he needs help" vs. "He knows how to have fun").

Yes, casual conversationalists may clarify their statements via colorful examples. One can infer from a story that a *boozer* is someone who consumes a large number of Jaeger bombs at a party or who engages in certain rambunctious activities when intoxicated. But in everyday life, one rarely hears a carefully conceived statement that explains what types of people (or activities, phenomena, etc.) do and do not merit a particular label. Are five drinks enough to act like a boozer? Is 10, 20, or 30? Similarly, we invoke the term *heavy drinker* without carefully distinguishing between other possible categories, such as *light, normal,* or *chronic* amounts of drinking. In ordinary conversations, such precision might seem overly formal, if not bizarre or annoying. Our conversational partners are usually content that they possess a "good enough" understanding what we mean and do not want or ask us for too many specifics.

Don't take my word for it. Do Exercise 3.1 a few times, and see for yourself. I think you'll find that people tend to use concepts in loose and casual ways in their everyday lives.[1] We usually do not define our terms (except

---

[1] See Garfinkel (1967, pp. 42–44) for a student exercise that makes a similar point. Garfinkel told his students to ask their everyday companions to clarify commonplace statements—for example, to ask whether "I'm tired" referred to mental or physical exhaustion or to tiredness felt in the muscles or bones and so on. Very quickly, students encountered annoyance and even hostility; in everyday life, the norm is to assume we understand "well enough" what our companions are talking about most of the time.

EXERCISE 3.1

The next time you have a conversation with friends, casually monitor the key adjectives or nouns that are used. (This can be done by subtly taking notes during or after the fact. These days, almost no one questions you when you type a few words on your phone.) Write down a few of the key terms that the participants used without defining, and then (later on) brainstorm some of the nuances that were overlooked.

If you're not a big talker, simply initiate a discussion of good or bad movies, television shows, or songs, and take note of the ambiguous nouns and adjectives your companions use as they discuss and debate these topics.

---

by example), and our companions rarely stop us from speaking vaguely or rashly. Most of the time, casual conversationalists (including myself) probably can't even formulate a coherent definition and can only claim, somewhat weakly, "I haven't worked out the details, but I know a heavy drinker when I see one!"

DEFINING CONCEPTS IN JOURNAL ARTICLES

Compared to most conversations, scholarly prose is carefully crafted. Each sentence may be labored over rather intensely. To be sure, scholars sometimes generate sentences that—like those spoken in conversations—are spontaneous and improvisational. But these sentences will be reread and (potentially) revised many times before finally appearing in print. As I explained in Chapter 2, scholars often devote many months to a single paper. They incorporate critical feedback from colleagues, collaborators, peer reviewers, copy editors, editors in chief, and others, all prior to publication. These efforts should be recognized and commended—especially in light of the ambiguous and ill-conceived claims that speakers regularly generate in ordinary life.

Not surprisingly, then, one finds carefully crafted definitions much more frequently in journal articles than in casual conversations. For example, in their article on "Predictors of College Students' Binge Drinking," Sun, Maurer, and Ho (2003) state on the very first page (and again in their methods section) that they are treating *binge drinking* as something that occurs when an individual has "five or more drinks in a sitting." Here, the authors attempt to convey a clear sense of the phenomenon that lies at the center of their analysis. It's helpful of them to do that, right? The concept of binge-drinking could signify many different things, and the authors have attempted to convey the sort of phenomenon they have in mind for the purposes of their paper.

Not all researchers are as conscientious. Researchers are not perfect. They don't always take the time to explain how they define important concepts. And, even when they do compose explicit definitions, their attempts are almost always flawed—helpful but flawed. As we'll see, many definitions tend to muddy things up nearly as much as they clarify. (If you're reading critically, then you might already be wondering about Sun et al.'s binge drinking example: But what is a *sitting*? And does a light beer count the same as a long island iced tea? What if one drinker weighs 100 pounds, while another weighs 250 pounds?)

First, let's discuss the range of options scholars have when it comes to defining key terms. You'll need to keep these options in mind as you search for the ambiguities that inevitably plague journal articles.

1) Sometimes authors neglect to define terms.

As authors get on with the complicated business of writing their papers, they often imagine that readers know "well enough" what they mean. Authors may assume that their readers are fellow scholars who already know and use the same definitions of technical terms like *message framing* or *satisficing*. Or, authors may assume that some concepts (such as *family* or *organization*) are so commonplace that virtually no reader would need assistance in comprehending them. Both assumptions can be wrong, of course—more on that further below. For now, let's simply look at an example of how authors use terms without defining them.

In an article on "Determinants of Parishioner Satisfaction Among Practicing Catholics," Peyrot and Sweeney (2000) study several factors that might shape how satisfied people are with the weekly church services they attend. Their first paragraph begins this way:

> Most research on religious beliefs and attitudes has had an institutional focus. Religious researchers have been more interested in how people relate to the broad doctrinal and ethical positions of their churches and denominations than in how they fit into their local congregations. Recently, a number of studies have begun to focus on the local context of the parish or synagogue since it is normally there that people have their primary religious experience and maintain a sense of identification with the larger institutional church. . . . (p. 209)

Peyrot and Sweeney (2000) do an admirable job setting up the topic of their paper: Most research has taken an "institutional approach," while they are contributing to a smaller and more recent body of work that examines the "local context." Here, they are locating their work within the field and are beginning to explain its potential contribution. No doubt they repeatedly revised these three sentences so that they could be as clear and accurate as possible.

Nevertheless, one could argue that they used important terms that went undefined. For example, in the third sentence, what does the phrase *primary religious experience* mean? Or, how about *identification*? Both of these concepts could be understood in many different ways, but the authors (rightly or wrongly) chose not to pause and define them.

Readers who are having trouble detecting any ambiguity might consider the following questions, which a critic could raise about the concept of primary religious experience: Does *primary* indicate that the experience is first (as in early in one's life), or that it is the most important, or both? What exactly is a *religious experience*? Does it include prayers that are said at home, school, or bedtime? Does it include attending church-affiliated schools and summer camps? Can seeing a beautiful rainbow be a religious experience? How about seeing the phrase "In God we trust" on a dollar bill? Are there such things as secondary and tertiary religious experiences, and, if so, where does one draw the line between them?

It is not necessarily a bad thing that Peyrot and Sweeney have glossed over such complexities. A plausible argument could be made that precise understanding of these terms is not essential to the authors' argument. Pausing to define them might unnecessarily delay and complicate the authors' work.

2) Sometimes authors implicitly define terms.

Another common practice is for authors to define terms implicitly, where a concept's meaning is conveyed more subtly and informally, without the stilted language of "I define 'X' as . . .". (Actually, if you reread that sentence, you'll notice that I attempted to define *implicitly* in an implicit fashion.)

In the above excerpt from Peyrot and Sweeney, take a look at how the concept *institutional* (used in the first sentence) was implicitly defined in the second and third sentences. A focus is institutional if it is concerned with the doctrinal and ethical positions of the church as a whole; it is contrasted with a more local focus that examines the experiences people have within their particular congregations.

Implicit definitions provide a useful and sometimes elegant strategy. Authors can convey a term's meaning without having to interrupt the smooth flow of their ideas. A paper with too many formal definitions ("I define 'X' as . . ." "I define 'Y' as . . ." I define 'Z' as . . .") might become tedious and boring without increasing clarity very much at all.

Researchers' implicit definitions are usually a vast improvement over the kinds of rash and imprecise statements that people make in everyday life. At the same time, even those most carefully crafted implicit definitions will usually contain numerous ambiguities.

3) Sometimes authors explicitly define terms.

The third option is for authors to define key concepts in a very clear and open fashion. Hopefully without overdoing it, an author may state "I define . . ." or "Here 'X' is defined as . . ." or use some other practical and explicit phrasing. Authors make different choices about how much valuable article space to spend on a definition: Some dash out a single sentence, others devote a paragraph, while (more rarely) others allocate multiple pages.

Here are two examples both focused on the same concept. First, Aksoy, Carter, and Wright (2012) provide a one-sentence definition of *terrorism* in the course of their article:[2]

> We utilize the following definition of terrorism: "the threatened or actual use of illegal force and violence by a non state actor to attain a political, economic, religious, or social goal through fear, coercion, or intimidation." (p. 811, n5)

In a second example, Gibbs (1989) provides a more detailed attempt to define this concept. He offers a five-part definition:

> Terrorism is illegal violence or threatened violence directed against human or nonhuman objects, provided that it
>
> 1. was undertaken or ordered with a view to altering or maintaining at least one putative norm in at least one particular territorial unit or population;
>
> 2. had secretive, furtive, and/or clandestine features that were expected by the participants to conceal their personal identity and/or their future location;
>
> 3. was not undertaken or ordered to further the permanent defense of some area;
>
> 4. was not conventional warfare and because of their concealed identity, concealment of their future location, their threats, and/or their spatial mobility, the participants perceived themselves as less vulnerable to conventional material action;
>
> 5. was perceived by the participants as contributing to the normative goal previously described [above] by inculcating fear of violence in persons (perhaps an indefinite category of them) other than the immediate target of the actual or threatened violence and/or by publicizing some cause. (p. 330)

---

[2] Quite reasonably, Aksoy et al. borrow this definition from the National Consortium for the Study of Terrorism and Responses to Terrorism.

Gibbs's article[3] has been reprinted in textbooks and cited many times. His work provides an impressive example of the seriousness with which social scientists treat the central terms of their analyses. Nevertheless, despite Gibbs's careful efforts, his lengthy definition of terrorism is still vague—as we'll see in the next section. Try though he might, Gibbs cannot completely eradicate the ambiguity of language. No scholar can.

TWO REASONS WHY CONCEPTS CAN BE CRITICIZED ☆

So far, we've seen that authors can take a range of approaches toward conveying the meaning of key terms. Scholars can neglect to define key concepts, assuming that readers know what those terms mean; scholars can provide implicit definitions, hoping that informal explanations in the surrounding text will sufficiently clarify what key terms mean; or scholars can provide explicit definitions that span a sentence, paragraph, or multiple pages.

The more careful and extensive the author is, the less room there is for ambiguity. Nevertheless, even in the best case scenario—where authors take the time to spell out an extensive and formal definition—ambiguity remains.

Let's look at two kinds of ambiguity that pervade virtually any article that appears in a social science journal.

1) Ambiguity and the dilemma of infinite regress

Let's assume the best case scenario—that an author has taken the time to provide an explicit and formal definition of a concept (as with our two terrorism examples). Any carefully conceived definition obviously involves words. It may be possible to provide a formal definition via a drawing, photograph, or symbol of some sort, but in journal articles, definitions come in the form of more words. And, quite perplexingly, those additional words seem to contribute as much mud as soap; they don't clean things up as well as one might expect.

The problem is that, as authors use words to define or clarify a concept, those explanatory words are also unclear and in need of explanation. As I mentioned earlier in a parenthetical comment, if *binge drinking* is defined as "five or more drinks in a single sitting," then what qualifies as a *drink* and as a *sitting*?

This has been called "the dilemma of infinite regress" (Agger, 2000), which is a fancy way of saying this: If I pause to define a key term, then I probably

---

[3] I should note that Gibbs's paper is conceptual and not empirical; he does not (strictly speaking) collect and analyze data but is focused entirely on creating an improved definition. Most journal articles cannot go into so much depth on a concept given space limitations and the other goals they hope to accomplish (e.g., presenting the findings of their analyses).

need to pause to define the new terms introduced by my definition, and then I need to define any additional words that appear in those new definitions, and so on. Presumably, scholars could infinitely regress or move backward forever as they attempt to define their way all the way back to some foundational concepts that need no clarification. Unfortunately, those words seem exceedingly rare, if they exist at all.

Let's return to Gibbs's work on terrorism. His lengthy, five-part definition is a praiseworthy attempt to bring specificity to an important, misused, and politically charged concept. (From watching the news or talking with friends, you might recall that drug dealers, spouse abusers, politicians, and others have been called "terrorists" in recent years.) Nevertheless, his definition invokes a number of terms whose meanings are far from clear. What exactly does Gibbs mean by *defense, furtive features, inculcating fear, norm, participant, publicizing, undertaken with a view,* and *violence?* Similar multipart definitions might be created for any of these terms, starting us down the path of infinite regress. To demonstrate, take a look at my attempt to further clarify one seemingly simple word that Gibbs invokes but does not define—*participant.*

A *participant* is someone who carries out a terrorist action (alone or with others), or who enables another or others to engage in a terrorist action

1. with knowledge of the purpose(s) of the activity

[This would help us exclude ignorant store clerks or other innocent people who unknowingly sell ammunition or bomb-making supplies to terrorists.]

2. who understand the nature and consequences of the activity

[This excludes participants' young children, who may not fully grasp what they're doing even if they are told of the purpose.]

3. without being forced to do so against their will

[This excludes hostages or blackmail victims but includes people exposed to peer pressure and other ordinary social forces like poverty and socialization.]

I think my attempt to clarify a key term in Gibbs's definition is pretty good, if I do say so myself. I made a genuine effort to further clean things up, but inevitably I have also introduced more muck. Someone could easily point out that I have introduced additional ambiguity that needs to be rectified: What exactly do I mean by *nature of the activity, against their will,* or even *will?*

If any definition could go on almost forever and contains no inherent stopping point to prevent us from the dilemma of infinite regress, then the stopping point any author does choose will be somewhat *arbitrary* (meaning things could easily be different). Definitions can always be made longer or shorter, but authors choose not to make them so. Researchers decide—while considering the opinions of editors, peer reviewers, and other audiences—that a particular number of paragraphs, or sentences, or words, or no discussion at all, is "good enough" for readers to "get the gist" of what a concept means.

The dilemma of infinite regress is only one issue that can be linked to arbitrariness—there are others. In the next section, I'll expand on the notion of arbitrariness by connecting it to researchers' disagreements over how to define key terms.

2) Arbitrariness and the lack of definitional consensus

Authors always have options when they invoke and define key terms. One choice they must make is whether to use, revise, or ignore definitions that have appeared in prior studies in the literature. An author may decide that a previously published definition is perfectly adequate, perhaps quoting an existing definition verbatim. Or, an author may dismiss and ignore an existing definition, considering it too flawed to use. Or, an author may attempt to improve a definition by adding new language or removing problematic language.

Across the social sciences, there is no centralized authority that tells authors "THIS is exactly how all researchers should define Concept X, now and forever—NO EXCEPTIONS!" Yes, shared understandings do arise in disciplines and subfields, and these may sometimes be enforced by reviewers and editors. Nevertheless, individual authors can usually exercise a great deal of discretion.

One way to critique a journal article, then, is to compare its definitions of key concepts to definitions that appear in other publications. This helps to show that the definition used by an author was not inevitable or objective because others defined the same concept differently. An author made a subjective choice in selecting a particular definition, and he or she could have chosen differently, like other authors have done. Also, keep in mind that competing definitions will usually have their own strengths and weaknesses. If you want to effectively critique a journal article, it can thus be very helpful to closely compare its definitions of key concepts with the definitions that other scholars have preferred to use.

As we have already seen, *terrorism* provides an example of a concept that is defined differently by different scholars: Aksoy et al. (2012) offered a one-sentence definition, and Gibbs (1989) advanced a much longer and more nuanced definition. These are not the only two definitions available. Schmid (1983) found more than 100 definitions of terrorism in the literature, and no moratorium on definition creation has been called since then. Jackson (2011) refers to the literature on terrorism as a "forest" that readers can get lost in as so many different authors have advanced so many debatable definitions.

You might think to yourself, "Perhaps *terrorism* is unique." I really don't think so. Every time I look into a new subfield in the social sciences, I find definitional discord surrounding key concepts.

In my first attempt at a major research project (Harris, 2006), I wanted to conduct a fairly exhaustive review of the literature on marital equality so that I could attempt to make an original contribution. I spent a couple years of my life reading and thinking about all the quantitative and qualitative research on the topic. One of the first things that became apparent to me was that there was no consensus regarding exactly what marital equality consisted of. Some scholars wrote as if marital equality meant sharing the household labor; others focused on the power to make important decision; others portrayed equality as a cost-benefit calculation, where spouses added up all the "good" and "bad" things (e.g., sense of humor, attractiveness, money) that they each brought to the marriage.

Some scholars would propose comprehensive, multifaceted definitions of marital equality, but these were never identical. Here are four examples of what I found:

- Haas (1980, p. 290) defined egalitarian marriages as "the sharing by husband and wife of each of the traditionally segregated family roles," including the breadwinner role, the domestic role, the handyman role, the kinship role, the child care role, and the major or minor decision-maker role.
- Steil (1997, p. 71) suggested that "relationship equality is a matter of attitudes and behaviors and process. Relationship equality involves equal participation in the responsibilities of the home, equal commitment to the responsibility to provide, equal voice in establishing priorities, and equal commitment to and investment in the work of relationships."
- Knudson-Martin and Mahoney (1998, p. 82) discerned "four characteristics of an equal relationship," including that "partners hold equal status; accommodation in the relationship is mutual; attention to the other in the relationship is mutual; and there is mutual well-being of partners."
- Schwartz (1994, p. 76), along with housework, decision making, and other elements, emphasized that "reciprocity in bed is one of the signature elements of equality in marriage."

In doing my literature review, I could see that there were some overlaps between authors' conceptions but many divergences and contradictions too. Moreover, when I looked closer at the key terms that appeared within scholars' definitions of equality—such as "sharing" labor or power—it did not appear that these were conceptualized clearly or consistently either (Harris, 2006; see also Chapter 5 in this book).

Again, you might think to yourself, "Perhaps *terrorism* and *marital equality* are both unusual examples." I doubt it. Of course, I can't claim to be familiar with all or even most of the key concepts that are used by social scientists. Yet, wherever I look, I tend to find definitional diversity. Consider these brief examples—I added some underlining to help you find key terms:

- Kroeber and Kluckhohn (1952, p. 291) counted almost 300 formal and informal definitions of <u>culture</u>.
- Burt (1980, p. 79), like Barnes (1972) before him, complained that the literature on network analysis resembles "a terminological jungle in which any newcomer may plant a tree."
- Pessen (1992, p. 363) suggested that "the number of definitions of <u>class</u> comes close to matching the number of scholars offering definitions. Not only do different schools of thought present their own definitions, but representatives of ostensibly the same school each tend to present a version that differs in some respects from the versions offered by others."
- van Brakel (1994) found that more than 20 competing definitions of <u>emotion</u> had been offered in the 1980s and early 1990s alone. Specific emotions (such as <u>anger</u>) had also been conceptualized in a wide variety of ways.
- Definitions of <u>family</u> tend to vary from author to author (Harris, S. R., 2008), with some scholars conceding that "a single, all-encompassing definition of 'family' may be impossible to achieve" (Erera, 2002, p. 3).
- Lewellyn (2002, p. 7) has suggested that "definitions of <u>globalization</u> are almost as legion as the number of experts on the subject."
- Coakley (2009, p. 6) has admitted that "when I say I study <u>sports</u>, people ask [what that concept includes]. . . . To respond is not easy, because there is no single definition that precisely identifies sports in all cultures in all times."

I present this list to support my argument that most social science concepts can (and often will) be given a variety of definitions. Still, you should notice that what I have just offered you is a very small sample of the thousands of concepts that social scientists use. So, don't take my word for it. Instead, investigate for yourself. When you encounter a definition in a journal article, you might skim through some other books and articles on the same topic to see if there is consistency and to contemplate what the strengths and weaknesses of different definitions may be.

CONCLUSION ☆

Let's recap the argument of this chapter. I started by suggesting that everyday conversationalists do a relatively poor job of defining their terms. We use concepts haphazardly, often without saying what we mean or even having a clear idea of what we mean. Few of our companions ask for clarification, for fear of appearing disagreeable or odd. When they do ask us for a definition, it is unlikely that we have a precise meaning in mind; instead, we'll likely give a spontaneous, improvisational, and vague answer.

In contrast, social scientists do spend a great deal of time thinking about their key concepts. They carefully write and rewrite their papers with the intention of being as clear and precise as possible. Prior to publication, manuscripts are read and critiqued by colleagues, peer reviewers, and editors who may further encourage authors to define or explain their key concepts.

Nevertheless, researchers are not perfect. All journal article use imprecise language. This chapter demonstrated two avenues for pursuing a critique.

First was "the dilemma of infinite regress" (Agger, 2000). We noted that, whenever an author offers a definition of a concept, that definition contains words that must be defined. If an author were to continue to define key terms and then define the words they use to explain their key terms, and so on, they would never get anything done. They would "move backward forever," chasing the mirage of clarity.

Second, whenever an author offers a definition of a concept, there is a strong likelihood that other scholars have used different definitions of the same term. In some cases, dozens or even hundreds of competing definitions can be found in the literature. Thus, one can consider what the potential strengths and weaknesses of competing definitions might be.

Exercise 3.2 offers a succinct list of questions that may help you apply the ideas from this chapter.

EXERCISE 3.2

Choose a journal article that interests you. Evaluate the way the authors attempted to define, or neglected to define, key terms.

a) Are there some important concepts that the authors could have defined but didn't? (Sometimes, authors neglect to provide even an implicit definition of a key term.)

b) Can you find a quote where the authors tried to explicitly or implicitly define one or two key concepts?

c) Can you explain why the authors' attempts to explicitly or implicitly define these terms are superior to what happens in ordinary conversations?

d) Can you critique one or two of the authors' explicit or implicit definitions like I did with Gibbs's definition of (a *participant* in) terrorism? In other words, can you provide a concrete example of the dilemma of infinite regress?

e) If you are ambitious, you might pursue this form of critique: Can you find another article (or book) that uses a different definition of the same key concept that appeared in the article you are evaluating? How do the two definitions contradict or differ from one another? What are the strengths and weaknesses of each of the definitions? (Your instructor or librarian may need to help you conduct a database search in order to accomplish this task.)

CHAPTER 4

LITERATURE REVIEWS

L ife is complicated, but that often doesn't stop people from speaking loudly and confidently about it. Radio talk show hosts have a real knack for pontificating at great lengths about a story they read in the news that morning. Sometimes our friends, family members, and coworkers can act equally self-assured and all knowing, even though they may simply be parroting a claim they heard on television or saw online. "Squawk! Have you heard the latest?"

Virtually anyone can participate in casual conversations. There is no peer review screening process, nor even an expectation that you have read anything about a topic before you make a claim or formulate an argument. Many people do keep abreast of current events via daily newspapers, monthly magazines, news websites like CNN.com, or (gods help us) Twitter and other random Internet sources. But—as I argued in Chapter 2—even serious journalism is usually a far cry from the scholarship produced by social researchers. The pre-pontificating background reading that laypersons do is usually pretty meager, regardless of whether they bother to peruse reputable news reports.

EXERCISE 4.1

The next time a friend or relative expresses a confident opinion about a social issue, try to make a few polite inquiries about the source of their knowledge. You could say, "Don't take this question the wrong way—this is something I have to do for class. From what sources did you learn about this issue? Have you read any serious books on this topic? Any peer-reviewed articles written by social scientists?"

In contrast, social researchers read—a lot. And it's quality reading, not just quantity. Before (and as) they engage in a project, researchers usually do an extensive review of the scholarly literature. They familiarize themselves with the latest books and articles on a topic, as well as "classic" works that have stood the test of time. Admittedly, reviewing the literature can involve some quick skimming; some books or articles may turn out to be minimally useful to one's project, after all. On the other hand, doing a lit review sometimes requires a slow, painstaking, line-by-line examination of densely complicated texts as scholars try to unpack the strengths, weaknesses, assumptions, and implications of prior work. (Students who have taken courses in social theory probably understand well what I am saying here. It can take half an hour to comprehend a single page of text written by a profound scholar.)

A journal article contains a reference section that lists the prior works that were cited in the paper. The list of books and articles can be quite long, but no matter how long, reference sections rarely include everything an article's author has read on the topic. Scholars read (and skim) much more than they end up citing. Why read so much? Authors don't want to simply parrot what an earlier scholar has said—and peer reviewers and editors usually won't let them. Instead, authors want their journal articles to advance their fields in some way. Authors need to familiarize themselves with the theories, methods, and findings of prior scholarship so that they can fill a neglected "gap" in the literature, overcome limitations in prior work, or make other kinds of positive contributions.

The work of a literature review can inform a scholar's entire research project. From past scholarship, researchers often derive and refine key concepts, hypotheses, sampling strategies, analytical techniques, solutions to ethical dilemmas, and other helpful ideas and practices.

Despite their wide-ranging impact, literature reviews are often associated with the introductory sections of a journal article—everything after the abstract and before the methodology section—because that is where scholars summarize prior research and explain how their article will add to it. In these introductory sections, much gets accomplished. Researchers expertly distill key points from the dozens or hundreds of prior studies that they have read; they identify competing perspectives, uncover important contradictions or disagreements that need to be resolved, and show the connections (and disconnects) between disparate studies—studies that may have been conducted decades apart by scholars in different disciplines and subfields.

I have a challenge for you: Pick a random journal article, and compare its (probably extensive) literature review with your findings from Exercise 4.1.

My guess is that this comparison will give you an appreciation for the amount of reading scholars do, and the work they put into synthesizing it, before they pontificate.

FINDING IMPERFECTIONS IN LITERATURE REVIEWS ☆

So far, I have argued that social scientists read more and read better than most laypersons. Casual conversationalists (like talk show hosts) are free to espouse opinions based on any tidbits of news they may hear. Researchers, in contrast, tend to read widely and deeply before formulating arguments and presenting them to an audience via journal articles.

We've thus established the first half of our guiding theme: Social research is superior to ordinary ways of knowing. Now it's time for the second half: recognizing the inevitable imperfections within social research.

While many weaknesses could be discussed, I will focus on three major dilemmas that all scholars face: selecting relevant publications from the literature, identifying what is relevant in any given publication, and interpreting the meaning of prior works.

1) What counts as relevant research?

Imagine you are a graduate student who is preparing to write a doctoral dissertation. And—lucky for you—you've developed a fairly passionate research interest early in your training. You have decided you want to study something about the factors influencing the migration of women from the Philippines to the United States. This seems a precise enough topic to start with and one that may eventually lead to a successful research project. As you formulated your topic and collected data to analyze, you would want to read the relevant literature. A dilemma would immediately arise for you, and it wouldn't go away.

The problem is that your research topic—like any research topic—is arguably related to literally hundreds of other similar subjects and to thousands of previous studies. Certainly much of the broad literature on gender might be germane because you have expressed an interested the factors influencing the migration of *women* from the Philippines to the United States. Much research on family and mothering could also be of interest because some Philippine women may be sending money back home to their own children, even while they help care for their employers' children. Relevant literatures could also be found in the areas of inequality and work because regional disparities and the pursuit of economic opportunity may be influencing Philippine women's decisions to seek employment outside their own country. Moreover, the Philippines may not prove to be an entirely unique case; as a serious student, you might want to read studies that examine migration to and from other regions (such as Europe or Latin America) in order to benefit from the insights, comparisons, and historical context that earlier research might provide. I could make similar arguments for the relevance of literatures on globalization, identity, race relations, decision making, emotion management, and many other topics.

A cornucopia of research on all of these potentially related topics could be found through a rigorous library search. As I write this, the database *Sociological Abstracts*—an electronic resource for locating journal articles—monitors more than 1,800 serials for content deemed relevant to sociology, with each outlet publishing hundreds or thousands of pages annually. And this list is by no means complete. Many helpful and relevant articles could also be found by searching databases associated with anthropology, economics, history, political science, psychology, women's studies, and so on. Plus, thousands of books are published each year in the social sciences. The existing literature is massive and constantly evolving; it could be described as a "blooming, buzzing confusion" (cf. James, 1890), especially for a novice researcher.

I could continue, but I think I have said enough to make my point: Drawing the line between the relevant and irrelevant literature is an arbitrary act. Researchers must be selective with their attention because they cannot possibly attend to all the previous literature that might be pertinent to their research projects. The manner in which authors exercise their selectivity has consequences: It shapes how they design their studies and interpret their results. It shapes what they think is known, what they try to find, and what they tell their readers.[1]

2) What is relevant within a publication?

Scholars' selective attention inevitably limits the number of published works that they choose to read and cite in their research projects. In addition, selectivity also operates at another level. Researchers usually can pay attention to and incorporate only a small amount of the information that appears within any given publication that they read.

An average article contains several thousand words. A careful reader could search all those words and find, undoubtedly, hundreds of discernible claims. Authors make claims related to the importance and extent of the

---

[1] Readers may want to connect this discussion with my critique of Sun et al.'s (2003) sampling in Chapter 6 and analysis in Chapter 7. In each chapter, some very similar skill sets are at work—imagining potentially relevant topics to read about and imagining other causal factors that may shape a dependent variable.

EXERCISE 4.2

Here is a potentially fun assignment—a scavenger hunt—that can help you begin to explore the selectivity of authors' literature reviews.

The first step is to choose a recently published journal article that interests you. Note the article's general subject (via the title and abstract) as well as its publication date. Then, perform a database search to locate an article on a similar topic that was published several years earlier. (If you don't know how to do a database search, your university librarian or your instructor should be happy to help you.) Read that article too. Can you make an argument that the author of the recent article could have benefitted from reading and citing the earlier article? Was there a concept, method, finding, or some other useful element from the earlier article that could have been explicitly incorporated into the recent article? Can you make a case that the earlier article really should have been included in the recent article or that it was at least as deserving of inclusion as some other references that the authors chose to include?

You might also report some quantitative results from your database search: How many dozens or hundreds of articles did you find that dealt with issues similar to the recent article—judging by the key terms appearing in titles and abstracts?

problem at hand, the nature of the existing literature, the available methods that have been and can be used to study the topic, the implications their findings have and the directions that future research should take, and so on. Any journal article puts forth numerous wide-ranging assertions. Thus, when reviewing a specific article (not to mention a book), scholars must choose what specific ideas to pay attention to and what ideas to filter out. The vast majority of what authors read (or skim) is not reflected in the final draft of their summaries of prior works. Authors must use their judgment— the best subjective judgment they can render—to decide what is relevant about any given article (or any given page of an article) for the purposes of their research projects.

For example, in my lengthy review of the quantitative literature on marital equality (Harris, 2000), I cited dozens of studies but used them in a highly selective fashion. I was primarily interested in comparing the different ways that scholars measured equality in marriage. I cited Piña and Bengtson's (1993) entire article in order to make a one-sentence point: that the authors "deem[ed] an equitable division of household labor to exist if husbands' and wives' contributions fall within seven hours per week of each other" (Harris, 2000, p. 123). I ignored Piña and Bengtson's theoretical perspective, their sampling strategy, the findings they generated, and other arguably important concerns. In crafting my review article, I made the subjective choice to ignore matters that I deemed nonessential to the task I had set for myself. Journal articles must be exceedingly concise and focused; authors (with guidance from peer reviewers and the editor) decide exactly how narrow that focus should be. But no matter where they end up drawing the line on what information to include, authors almost never have space to give full and fair summaries of the articles they cite.

If authors make selective use of previous journal articles, then this is at least doubly true of their treatment of books. Consider one important book—Weber's *Economy and Society*—which has been cited more than 12,000 times (according to Google Scholar). This impressive tome is full of insight. However—at 1,467 pages—it can really weigh down your backpack. No journal article could do justice to the full range and complexity of the ideas that appear on those pages. Any standard literature review treatment could be deemed a highly superficial discussion of Weber's book—there's almost no way around it.

For example, in their article "Power and the Perception of Social Networks," Simpson, Marvoksky, and Steketee (2011) cite *Economy and Society* as an important theoretical resource. How many sentences do you think they spent in their discussion of that thick book? About three. They credit Weber with two ideas: the first that "power has many correlates such as status and wealth" and the second that "the beliefs of those at the top of power and prestige orders are more likely to influence the behavior of others than the beliefs of those with lower status" (Simpson et al., 2011, pp. 166, 170).

A critical reader can look at this breezy literature review and ask, Did Weber have other important ideas about power that could be applied to Simpson et al.'s article? What might Weber (whose methodology might be described as historical) have thought of the authors' data collection and analysis (which involved conducting experiments with undergraduates)? Did Weber define *power* in the same way that Simpson et al. do, or are there important differences?

These sorts of questions cannot be entertained in the rapid-fire pace of social science journal articles. Authors may make Herculean efforts to read and learn from prior research—and they are to be applauded for those efforts—but they must inevitably ignore or gloss over much of the information that is contained in those past works. The case of *Economy and Society* is an extreme example, but it helps illustrate my general point.

EXERCISE 4.3

Here is another scavenger hunt assignment.

First, choose a relatively recent journal article that interests you—it can be the same article you started with in Exercise 4.2. Then, look at the reference section and pick out an interesting publication the author cited. Obtain a copy of this publication (preferably by downloading it from your library's website), and read it for yourself.

Is there any important information that the authors left out when they cited this previous publication? Does the earlier publication contradict the authors' article in any way that the authors neglect to mention? Are there differences in theoretical orientations, conceptual definitions, measurement strategies, or findings? Can you make an argument that the authors used information from the earlier publication in a selective (or even somewhat misleading) fashion?

---

3) What does the existing literature mean?

In Chapter 1, we discussed various manifestations of ordinary human inquiry as opposed to social research. One of those manifestations was the practice of consulting a sacred text in order to make sense out of social life. Believers cite or quote the Bible, the Koran, the Book of Mormon, or other religious documents not only to discuss otherworldly matters but to make claims about human affairs. What is the best way to form a family? Is homosexuality a healthy sexual orientation? Is abortion, euthanasia, slavery, or warfare ever justifiable? Thus, a 2,000-year-old passage in the Bible can be used to promote marriages where the husband leads and the wife follows, or a 1,400-year-old passage in the Koran can be invoked to justify the need for women to wear a veil in public.

Interestingly, religious texts are always open to multiple interpretations. Liberal believers can read the same text and draw different inferences than their conservative counterparts do. Some Christians infer from St. Paul's letter to the Ephesians that women should be equal partners in marriages, and some Muslims treat the Koran as saying that veiling is not mandatory for women (Bartkowski & Read, 2003). Believers can debate the translation of key words, the meanings of phrases and sentences, the necessity of reading the text literally, figuratively, as a product of its historical context, and so on.

Given the theme of this book—that research is better than ordinary human inquiry yet far from perfect—there are two comparisons I would make between the use of texts by the religious and use of literature reviews by social scientists.

Any Text Can Be Criticized and Overturned

First, here's a key difference: Social scientists seem somewhat less likely to treat the truth as something eternally established by any key text. In empirical journal articles, social scientists want to test out ideas, reject or revise outdated ideas, develop new theories, and so on. Scholars are not beholden to the eternal legitimacy of any one text; they are encouraged to develop and propose new truths at every turn and to justify those truths via careful examination of data. Thus, rather than simply claiming that the Bible says (in some passages) that marriage should be between one man and one woman, social scientists are more likely to attempt to collect data on testable research questions, such as "Do children raised by heterosexual parents exhibit a smaller or larger number of behavioral troubles than children raised by same-sex parents?" (e.g., see Patterson, 2006). Any social science book or article—even those written by founding figures of the discipline—is liable to be critiqued or overturned without fear of sanction. In fact, it's quite the opposite: Kudos go to social scientists who radically reshape how their disciplines approach a particular topic.

Arguably, the willingness to critically scrutinize, test out, and overturn ideas (rather than accepting them on faith) is something that is much more common in journal articles than in everyday life.[2] I would call it a strength of research—another way social science is (arguably) better than ordinary human inquiry.

Any Text Can Be Interpreted in Different Ways

My second comparison focuses on the imperfections that researchers share with ordinary human inquiry. I have always found it fascinating (even humorous) how debates between social scientists can sound so similar to religious debates over authoritative texts. Just as there are interpretive camps within religious communities, so too are there within the social sciences. Scholars often do not agree with each other on what the previous literature means. A book, an article, a paragraph, a sentence, a concept—all these and more can be interpreted in different ways by different scholars (e.g., see Fine & Kleinman, 1986; Harris, 2010).

In my experience as an author, journal editor, and reader of the literature, I have seen many times how social scientists can adopt different and

---

[2] Careful readers will notice that I am indicating that the difference is a matter of degree and is not all or nothing. It is definitely possible to find ideas that researchers sometimes take on faith, such as the notions that people have free will, that people do not have free will, and so on.

contradictory viewpoints on the same piece of scholarship. It's not just that psychologists disagree with sociologists or that political scientists disagree with anthropologists. And it's not just that subfields can be in contention—as when culturally oriented psychologists disagree with biologically oriented psychologists. Scholars may be trained in the same discipline, and they may work in the same subfield, and they may even share the same theoretical and methodological preferences, yet they may still disagree radically on fundamental questions about the existing literature. And by *fundamental*, I mean questions like "Is that article good, mediocre, or horrible?" "What, if any, cumulative knowledge has been produced on a particular topic over the past few decades?" And, as we already saw in Chapter 3, "What's the best way to define the central terms of our analyses?" For any of these questions, answers can vary across disciplines, across camps within disciplines, across subcamps within camps, and so on.

Disagreement starts in the peer review process. In evaluating a manuscript, editors usually seek out peer reviews from two, three, or four experts. As we discussed in Chapter 2, editors keep reviewers' identities confidential in order to encourage brutally honest and critical evaluations. Reviewers usually provide two or three pages of typed feedback outlining what they see as the strengths and weaknesses of a manuscript; they also render judgments about whether they think an article should be accepted outright (which rarely happens), rejected outright (which sometimes happens), or considered again after revisions have been made (which often happens). Disagreements can and usually do arise as some reviewers advise editors to reject, while others recommend to accept with minor changes or invite authors to make major changes and resubmit. Even when reviewers adopt the same general stance toward a paper, they disagree on the details: One may think a particular methodological strategy is strong, but another thinks it's weak, and so on. An editor may also have his or her own thoughts on the paper. All of these diverse views must be considered as an author strives to compose an article that is "good enough" for an editor, ultimately, to accept. It can be difficult, of course, to accommodate commentators who have incompatible evaluations of a manuscript. (Ask your professors about it; they probably have entertaining horror stories to tell.)

After articles (and books) survive the rigorous review process, they are still far from perfect—they are not immune to further criticism and disagreement by scholars who read, cite, and discuss them.

Consider two renowned works: Foucault's (1979) *Discipline and Punish* and Hochschild's (1983) *The Managed Heart*. Each book has been cited thousands of times and is widely considered to be profound and groundbreaking, yet each has been subjected to harsh criticism. Von Schriltz (1999, p. 410) claimed that Foucault was wrong "in virtually every major detail," and Wouters (1989, pp. 112, 119–120) asserted that Hochschild wrote an "irritating" and "exaggerated" book that lacked an adequate theoretical framework. My own, infinitely less-influential research (Harris 2001, 2006) has been praised as beneficial reading for all social scientists (Kettlitz, 2008) and as a prime example of what researchers should not do[3] (Kleinman & Kolb, 2011).

Not only do scholars sometimes disagree about the quality of prior work, but the message or implications of a text are also matters of interpretation. For example, Herbert Blumer (1969) coined the phrase *symbolic interaction* to refer to a theoretical perspective that has influenced disciplines of sociology and communication, among others. Compared to most founding figures, Blumer's writing is exceedingly clear and straightforward. Nevertheless, disagreements arise about his perspective. Some say Blumer disdained quantitative methodologies, whereas others say he likes them just fine (see Ulmer, 2001). Some say Blumer advocated an approach that focuses on the *micro level* (face-to-face level) of social interaction, whereas others say Blumer dealt rigorously with larger-level, *macro* issues (see Maines, 1988). In literature reviews, as in most things, opinions vary.

☆ CONCLUSION

Let's recap. I started this chapter by arguing that people don't read very much in everyday life. In comparison, social scientists read more, and what they read is better—peer-reviewed, scholarly research. Scholars should be commended for reading (potentially) hundreds of books and articles as they engage in their own projects. Their research benefits immensely from the intense literature reviews that they conduct.

Nevertheless, scholars are imperfect. They cannot read everything. And, when they do read prior publications, they ignore information that does not neatly fit their interests and agendas. Hence, researchers are doubly selective—selecting from the literature at large and selecting what to pay attention to within any given article or book.

Alongside imperfections of selection, scholars must interpret what they read. They render subjective judgments about the quality and the implications of past work. Literature reviews are not simply objective portraits of fields but can be seen as stories that authors tell from their own perspectives (Agger, 2000). Researchers (with feedback from editors and peer

---

[3] Interestingly, I received a prestigious honor (The Cooley Award) from the Society for the Study of Symbolic Interaction (SSSI) in 2011, the same year that the journal associated with the SSSI published an article lambasting my research.

reviewers) make subjective decisions about how to characterize the prior work that they have chosen to cite in the limited journal space that they are allotted.

If you are a newcomer to the world of journal articles, then literature reviews can seem overwhelming: dense prose, dozens of citations to prior research that you probably have not read, objective-sounding summaries written by smart individuals with PhDs. Who are we, mere readers, to disagree with what the experts say about the literatures they have reviewed?

Yet, in this chapter, I have suggested that a persistent reader can launch a meaningful critique of virtually any literature review. Even the most technically sophisticated article can be challenged for its selective and interpretive treatment of prior works. Exercise 4.4, along with the three earlier exercises, provides some guidance on how to put this chapter's ideas into practice.

EXERCISE 4.4

From Exercise 4.3, you should have one relatively recent article (let's call it RA) and one earlier article (let's call it EA) that was published several years prior. The authors of RA cited and discussed EA. Your mission—should you choose to accept it—is to critically evaluate what the authors of RA said about EA. You have two options:

1. **Make an argument that the authors of RA actually misinterpreted EA.** Did the authors of RA characterize EA in a way that you can reasonably disagree with? For example, did the authors of RA describe EA as

   • about topic X, but you think EA is more about topic Y?
   • a solid piece of scholarship but (in your opinion) EA has fatal flaws?
   • a weak piece of scholarship, but (in your opinion) EA has many strengths?

   These bullet points are merely suggestions; if you are creative, you might come up with additional arguments you could make.

2. **Make an argument that different scholars have interpreted EA differently.** To do this, use Google Scholar (or another database) to find a few more articles that also cite EA. Download them. Search within these recent articles (electronically, if possible) in order to find the pages on which the authors of EA are mentioned. Read carefully, and determine if EA is characterized inconsistently across RA and all of your other recent articles. Warning: This option may take a few attempts and could be challenging!

CHAPTER 5

MEASUREMENT

In Chapter 3, we discussed *conceptualization*—how authors define key terms in their research. This chapter focuses on *operationalization*—how authors measure things. Researchers develop specific procedures for detecting social phenomena: Do students have low or high self-esteem? How popular is a politician with the public? Are spouses dividing up household chores fairly? To address these sorts of questions, researchers do not simply need definitions of concepts like self-esteem or popularity or marital inequality; they need a system for investigating how much esteem or popularity or inequality actually exists.

In keeping with the theme of this book, let's briefly compare the "measurements" people take in everyday life to those undertaken by social scientists. Then we'll focus on the imperfections that pervade social research.

OPERATIONALIZATION IN EVERYDAY LIFE

In everyday life, people tend to measure things in casual and offhand ways. For example, my students sometimes say, "It's freezing in this classroom!" In this case, they may have "measured" the temperature by simply sensing its effect on their skin rather than looking at the more precise reading that a thermostat might display. Or, consider how a person may eat a jalapeño and proclaim, "That's a very spicy pepper," based on the burning sensation on his or her tongue; in contrast, a more scientific approach would be to measure the amount of capsaicin present and then rate the pepper's spiciness via the Scoville scale.[1]

---

[1] Go ahead and Google the words *Scoville* and *peppers*. You'll find figures like these:
- Banana peppers contain 1,000 to 2,500 Scoville heat units.
- Jalapeños contain 3,500 to 8,000 Scoville heat units.
- Habaneros contain 100,000 to 350,000 Scoville heat units.

Beware the habanero—now that's a very spicy pepper!

People also use relatively informal procedures to assess social phenomena, such as the personalities of our friends, relatives, coworkers, and acquaintances. By casually observing our companions, we try to measure the degree to which they are compassionate, lazy, hardworking, shy, gluttonous, hard-core partiers, and so on. We look for examples and treat them as indicators—as signs that a particular quality is present. Did Mary take time to comfort a friend? Did she get "totally drunk" recently? We look for evidence and classify people according to the impressions they make on us.

As casual observers, our measurements are not very systematic or impartial. We tend to create a mental image—a prejudice of sorts—and then look for evidence that confirms our expectations. For example, many Americans (including me) watched President George W. Bush for any statement or action that indicated a low level of intelligence. Did he use improper grammar? Did he try to exit a news conference via a locked door? More recently, many Americans have scrutinized Vice President Joseph Biden's behavior in order to discover indicators that he is gaffe prone. Did you hear that Biden referred to Obama as "articulate" and "clean"? Did you see the news story where Biden mistakenly asked someone in a wheelchair to "stand up and be recognized by the audience"?

The more indicators we can assemble, the more convinced we grow about our classifications. We may confidently tell others what we think ("Bush is so dumb—he may be the stupidest president in U.S. history"), or we may repeat our opinions to ourselves, silently or under our breath ("Gosh, that Mary is the most kindhearted person I know" or "Biden—he's such a gaffe machine").

As we'll see, researchers try to do better than this, but they are far from perfect.

☆ SCHOLARS' MEASUREMENTS ARE (USUALLY) BETTER THAN LAYPERSONS'

Researchers collect data in a variety of ways. For example, they may ask respondents a series of questions via a survey (as your instructors do via teaching evaluations); they may examine news coverage of an issue over time, performing content analysis; they may observe social interaction (in person or via video) and analyze what they see as part of an experimental design or as part of an ethnographic project. A general research methods textbook is a good place to get an overview of the broad array of strategies social scientists use to obtain and analyze data (e.g., Babbie, 2010).

In this section, I will not weigh all the pros and cons of the various strategies that researchers employ to collect data and take measurements. Instead,

I will make three simple points to support my argument that scholarly measurements—especially (but not only) those that appear in quantitative journal articles—tend to be superior to the measurement systems used in everyday life.

1) Social scientists carefully think through how best to measure something. Before and as researchers complete a study, they consider and compare different ways to gauge the degree to which a phenomenon exists. By doing a literature review, scholars read about the measurement techniques that have (or have not) worked well for scholars in the past. In the literature, researchers openly discuss and debate measurement strategies and try to improve upon past work when possible. There are even specialized journals that cater to papers that are focused on measurement and other methodological issues. Some of these outlets are interdisciplinary, such as the *International Journal of Social Research Methodology*; others are disciplinary, such as *Psychological Methods, Sociological Methods and Research,* and the *International Journal of Research & Method in Education*.

2) Scholars usually attempt to use consistent, systematic measurement procedures throughout a study.

In everyday life, we might be tempted to measure intelligence one way for a president we like and another way for a president we don't like. We may be tempted to treat a grammatical mistake as a trivial error on one occasion and as irrefutable proof of "stupidity" on another occasion. We can do this because we have not articulated a specific and fair set of procedures that will be used to identify and weigh indicators of intelligence. Researchers (usually) try to do better than that.

Let's return to Sun et al.'s (2003) study of binge drinking for an example. Like intelligence, ordinary conversationalists may have no clear idea of how to measure a person's level of binge drinking, which leads them to rely on haphazard observations as they classify whether or how often their companions over-imbibe. Sun et al., on the other hand, employed a specific procedure that was consistently applied to every student (more than 1,000) in their sample. They employed a survey question that had been used successfully by many researchers before them.

Think back over the last two weeks. How many times have you had five or more drinks[2] at a sitting?

---

[2] On the survey, there is an asterisk next to the word *drinks* with a footnote indicating that "*A drink is a bottle of beer, a glass of wine, a wine cooler, a shot glass of liquor, or a mixed drink."

- o None
- o Once
- o Twice
- o 3 to 5 times
- o 6 to 9 times
- o 10 or more times

This sort of questioning does rely on respondents' memory of and honesty about their own past behavior—both of which may be problematic. And, it includes ambiguous language, such as the term *sitting*. Nevertheless, a survey question such as this can be seen as a careful attempt to collect data in an objective and systematic fashion. The question is relatively simple, clear, and succinct. It treats everyone in the sample fairly without playing favorites like we might do in everyday life. It efficiently measures whether (and how often) students binge drink without taking too much time or effort on the part of researchers or respondents.

3) Researchers tell their readers exactly how they measured something so that others can find flaws or propose better measures.

In everyday life, we may never tell others (or even be able to tell ourselves) how we are measuring something like intelligence or binge drinking. In contrast, scholars try to make their measurement choices explicit. The methods sections of journal articles often describe the exact procedures that researchers used to measure each variable; readers can thus better understand how the study was done and how it might be done better. For instance, someone might argue that a different wording would improve the question that Sun et al. (2003) used to measure binge drinking, leading to the collection of more accurate data in a subsequent study.

These three brief points do not constitute an exhaustive list, but they are enough to support my general argument: Social scientists take measurement seriously, and they should be commended for their efforts. Researchers tend to measure things more carefully, systematically, and explicitly than people do in everyday life. Don't take my word for it—try Exercise 5.1 a few times and see for yourself.

☆ CRITIQUING MEASURES

Although researchers tend to put a great deal of thought into their measurement systems, the results are far from perfect. There is often no one best way to gauge the degree to which a social phenomenon exists. Instead,

EXERCISE 5.1

1. **Find a couple standard quantitative journal articles; they can be the same ones you used in the exercises for Chapters 3 and 4.** Take a close look at the methods sections to see if the authors describe the procedures they used to measure key concepts or variables in their studies. Then, think about how these same concepts might be measured in everyday life. Can you make an argument that the social scientists put more thought and effort into their measurement systems than ordinary people probably would?

2. **Find a recent textbook on research methods at your university library, such as Babbie (2010).** Read the chapter (or sections) on operationalization. Make a list of three ideas or strategies that reflect social scientists' greater concern with careful measurement compared to the concern laypeople exhibit.

researchers must choose from a wide range of options, all with advantages and disadvantages. As a result, different researchers tend to employ different strategies to measure "the same" phenomenon.

Imagine you want to measure your body weight to see if you are getting fatter over time. You're a fully grown adult and aren't getting any taller. You have choices: You might step on a bathroom scale, you might put on an old pair of pants to see how well they fit, or you might jump into a swimming pool to see how large of a splash you make on the surrounding patio. Some of these strategies may seem better than others. You might even pick one strategy and then use it repeatedly year after year to see if your weight has changed. It may seem most sensible to write down your bathroom-scale weight every January 1 to track your progress over the years.

If you switched measurement systems yearly—using the pants method one year, the swimming pool method the next, and the bathroom scale in another—then it would be more difficult to compare the results of your inquiries from year to year. Thus, a reasonable person might be tempted to stick to a single method to make the results comparable over time. This sounds great, but there's a dilemma: What if you chose a "weak" method early on (e.g., the swimming pool method) and you wanted to make a genuine improvement in your measurement system?

You've arrived at a dilemma: Using a consistent measurement allows for easier comparisons across separate studies; however, changing a measurement may help improve its effectiveness. Which route do you choose?

Scholars face this dilemma all the time, and they make different judgment calls about it. Sometimes, they are content to reuse existing measures (developed by themselves or by prior scholars), while other times, they want to innovate and improve on existing measures. As researchers debate which measures are better—the new ones or the old ones—additional new-and-improved instruments continue to be created and used in journal articles, giving future scholars even more options to choose from.

The proliferation of inconsistent measures—sometimes called *discontinuity*—offers us at least two ways of critiquing journal articles.

First, if we realize that authors often have many options when they measure something, then we can question the choices they make. We can ask, Would their research have been stronger if a different measure had been used? What are the strengths and weaknesses of a particular measure in comparison to one or more measures that a researcher chose not to use?

Second, researchers' use of inconsistent measures can allow us to ask deeper and more challenging questions about the utility and value of research over time: If scholars frequently use inconsistent measures, then is their research comparable and cumulative? Are different scholars studying the same thing, and can their research findings be combined into a coherent set of implications, facts, or lessons about the social world?

Let's explore measurement discontinuity by considering the topics of binge drinking and marital equality, followed by a shorter discussion of several miscellaneous examples.

Measuring Binge Drinking

Recall Sun et al.'s (2003) measurement system: They asked respondents (via a paper-and-pencil questionnaire) to answer the question: "How many times have you had five or more drinks at a sitting?" While many social scientists have adopted similar techniques to study binge drinking, their approaches are not entirely consistent. In fact, there is a large amount of discontinuity in research on this topic.

For instance, scholars make different choices regarding the time frame. When reflecting on drinking behavior, researchers sometimes ask respondents to think about the past week, or the past month, or the past six months, or the past year (see Courtney & Polich, 2009). These are not necessarily trivial decisions; different measures can produce different results and are thus a matter of debate. One advantage of using a shorter time frame is that respondents can better remember their recent behavior; a disadvantage is that the short time period may be anomalous. If I ask, "How many times did you binge drink?" during two weeks that include spring or summer break, your answer may be much different than if I ask you about the two weeks that precede your final exams. Students' drinking is likely to vary during different times of the year.

Scholars also differ on the number of drinks that constitute a binge. Some prefer to use "five in a sitting" (like Sun et al., 2003), but there is no consensus on that number or that phrasing. Some prefer to use four drinks for women to accommodate their lower metabolisms; some prefer to ask more precisely about drinks per hour rather than using the language of *sitting* or *occasion;* some argue that drinkers' body weights need to be measured and taken into account (see Courtney & Polich, 2009).

Moreover, various labels and distinctions can be found in the literature reflecting different definitions and different methodological choices. Sun et al. (2003) treated all their binge-drinking respondents the same; it didn't matter if respondents binge drank once, five times, or ten times in the past two weeks—they were all placed into the same category and then compared (statistically) to those who never binge drank. In contrast, some researchers do choose to distinguish between different kinds of binge drinkers. Read, Beattie, Chamberlain, and Merrill (2008) chose to distinguish between "lower-level binge drinkers" (e.g., males who drank five or six drinks in a sitting) and "heavy binge drinkers" (e.g., males who drank seven or more drinks). Meanwhile, Kokavec and Crowe (1999) decided to draw a line between "regular drinkers"—who consume at least ten drinks every day—and "binge drinkers"—who consume at least ten drinks but no more than two days per week.

When it comes to binge drinking, there are a plethora of strategies for measuring and parsing the phenomenon, with many more techniques created with each passing decade.[3]

Measuring Marital Equality

Researchers have been studying equality in marriage for several decades, but scholars have not achieved consensus regarding how best to measure the phenomenon. Many scholars have focused on sharing household labor as the most important dimension of marital equality, as opposed to power, respect, sexual relations, communication, or other factors. Yet, even among scholars who focus on labor, there is no standard set of procedures for measuring whether, or to what degree, couples are "sharing" the labor. Instead, many dozens (if not hundreds) of different procedures have been pursued.

---

[3] Some commentators note that a *binge* historically referred to very heavy drinking that spanned the course of multiple days (e.g., going on a three-day binge). See Best (2008, pp. 38–39) and Herring, Berridge, and Thom (2008).

One of the earliest and most influential attempts was Blood and Wolfe's (1960) survey research. To measure the division of labor, Blood and Wolfe employed a questionnaire that asked respondents a series of eight "Who usually . . .?" questions: Who usually washes the dishes, does the grocery shopping, mows the lawn, keeps track of money and bills, and so on. To answer, participants could choose from five options: "husband always" (1), "husband more than wife" (2), "husband and wife exactly the same" (3), "wife more than husband" (4), and "wife always" (5). By assigning quantitative values to these responses—which I put in parentheses—and adding up the scores for each chore, Blood and Wolfe (1960) created a numerical representation of the degree of inequality in respondents' marriages. A high score would indicate a marriage where the wife was doing more of the household labor, whereas a low score would indicate that the husband was doing more. For example, if the "wife always" did each of the eight chores, the score would be 40 (8 x 5 = 40). If the "husband always" did each chore, the score would be 8 (8 x 1 = 8).

In subsequent decades and across hundreds of journal articles and books, Blood and Wolfe's (1960) system has been slightly tweaked, radically revised, or cast aside entirely (see Warner, 1986; Shelton & John, 1996; Harris, 2006). I'll mention just four areas of discontinuity.

First, researchers have disagreed with Blood and Wolfe's (1960) list of questions—perhaps dropping lawn mowing but adding other chores like disciplining the children. Thus, the original list of chores not only changes but increases or decreases in size: For example, Goldberg, Smith, and Perry-Jenkins (2012, p. 818) collected data on 27 tasks, whereas Geist and Cohen (2011, p. 835) focused on only three key tasks.

Second, many scholars have focused solely on spouses' labor and do not allow respondents to indicate whether a third person (such as a child, relative, or hired help) sometimes or always does a particular chore (e.g., Blood & Wolfe, 1960; Hank & Jürges, 2007). Other scholars do include the third-party response option but process it differently. For example, Geist and Cohen (2011) treated tasks done by third parties as being "shared equally" between spouses—giving the husband and wife equal credit for the chore. However, Lewin-Epstein, Stier, and Braun (2006) argued that women often supervise third-party contributions to household labor, and so they chose to treat third-party tasks as "wife mostly responsible."

Third, many scholars have followed Blood and Wolfe's (1960) lead and collected data from only one spouse in each marriage. It is obviously cheaper and more efficient to gather data from a single spouse rather than both. However, this measurement strategy begs a question: Should one person's interpretation be treated as an adequate portrayal of a marriage (e.g., see Safilios-Rothschild 1969)? A smaller number of scholars collect data from both husbands and wives. This seems meritorious but raises another thorny question: What should be done when there are discrepancies between husbands' and wives' descriptions of their marriages? Researchers respond in different ways. For example, Hank and Jürges (2007) decided to use the average of spouses' estimates of their household labor—splitting the difference—whereas Lee and Waite (2005) kept spouses' estimates separate.

A fourth area of discontinuity in the marital equality literature involves a (deceptively) straightforward question: What counts as close enough for a marriage to be classified as equal? It was this discontinuity that helped motivate my own research on marital equality (Harris, 2000, 2006). I noticed that some measurement systems treated husbands as "egalitarian" if they did at least 40 percent of the housework (Haas, 1980; Smith & Reid, 1986), whereas other systems drew the line at 45 percent (Hochschild, 1989, p. 282). I also noticed that some researchers set hourly cutoff points instead of using percentages. Piña and Bengtson (1993, p. 905) decided that equality had been achieved if spouses' contributions were within seven hours per week of each other (e.g., he does 13 hours, and she does 20). In another study (Benin & Agostinelli, 1988, p. 353), researchers classified as equal those marriages where husbands and wives both did between 16 and 20 hours of housework per week. Blumstein and Schwartz (1983, pp. 144-145), meanwhile, employed a cutoff point of 11 to 20 hours per week and counted couples as egalitarian if both spouses fell within that range. As you can see, the same marriage might be classified as either equal or unequal, depending on the particular measurement system that a researcher chose to employ.

Thus, similar to research on binge drinking, many discontinuities pervade the literature on marital equality. Scholars invent measures, innovate upon them, and never settle on a single, consistent system. And while some measurement choices may in fact be better than others, I think you can see that none is perfect. Rather, scholars must select from flawed options as they attempt to be careful, systematic, and explicit about their measurement strategies.

Miscellaneous Examples

No one—including me—can claim to have read more than a tiny fraction of the vast amount of social research that scholars have produced. Nevertheless, my sense is that the subfields of binge drinking and marital equality are not unique. From what I have seen, discontinuity pervades research on most topics across the social sciences. Consider these miscellaneous examples:

- Researchers published 16 articles on aspiration and used 16 different measurement strategies in just a five-year period (Bonjean, Hill, & McLemore, 1965).
- By the late 1980s, social scientists had developed more than 200 ways to measure self-esteem (Scheff, Retzinger, & Ryan, 1989; see also Blascovich & Tomaka, 1991).
- Researchers have created hundreds of instruments for measuring the concept of quality of life (Gladis, Gosch, Dishuk, & Crits-Christoph, 1999).
- Twenty-five years after the initial development of a widely used measure of gender identity—the Bem Sex Role Inventory—researchers had not settled on a particular set of questions or a consistent procedure for scoring respondents' answers (Hoffman & Borders, 2001).
- Prejudice has been measured in a myriad of ways, each with strengths and weaknesses, giving researchers a large number of diverse options to choose from (Olson, 2009).

Still, don't simply accept my argument on faith. Discontinuity may not be universal—and, it is likely to be more pronounced in some areas of research compared to others. I encourage you to complete Exercise 5.2 and see how much discontinuity (if any) exists in whatever subfields interest you the most.

Remember, the goal of this book is not for you to simply memorize a set of facts or opinions. Rather, I hope to instill in you a healthy respect for social science research while at the same time providing you a set of concepts and questions that can be used to find the imperfections that pervade most journal articles.

☆ CONCLUSION

I started this chapter by arguing that laypersons are not very careful, systematic, or explicit in how they measure things. People draw inferences about what someone is like or what is going on based on very casual observations. Ironically, this enables us to say things like "President Bush is so dumb" while using measurement systems that are, arguably, pretty feeble.

In contrast, I argued, social scientists do better. They think through their measurement strategies and purposefully employ a particular set of procedures. They read about the instruments that have been used in prior research and consider whether to adopt or adapt these techniques. Researchers inform their readers exactly how key variables were measured so that others can learn from their successes and mistakes.

Unfortunately, there is rarely one best way to measure something. Instead, there are usually many options, each with advantages and disadvantages, and scholars often don't achieve consensus regarding what set of operational procedures will best gauge whether, and to what degree, a phenomenon exists. Thus, measures can be criticized for being weaker than or incomparable to the available alternatives.

Once again, this chapter has affirmed the tone and thesis of my book: Journal articles should be read with due respect for the time, effort, and expertise that went into them. Yet, articles should be approached with a healthy dose of skepticism, as virtually any piece of research can be critiqued for the methodological choices that its authors made. Exercise 5.2 offers a set of questions that may help you get started practicing the ideas from this chapter.

EXERCISE 5.2

Find an article that measures a phenomenon you are interested in. Self esteem, quality of life, and prejudice are options, or you might use an article you found for the exercises in Chapters 3 or 4.

1. **What do you think of the measurement strategy the authors used?** Do you see any obvious strengths or weaknesses? Can you argue that the authors could have done something different or better? Do the authors themselves mention measurement choices they considered but decided not to use—and, if so, what are the pros and cons of the various alternatives?

2. **For a challenging scavenger hunt, find additional articles that measure the same phenomenon.** How much, if at all, do the authors' measurement strategies differ? Are there potential advantages or disadvantages to the different measures that the different researchers used?

It could be challenging for a beginner to find multiple articles that measure the same phenomenon. You will have to search (with guidance from your instructor or librarian, if needed) a database such as *Sociological Abstracts* or *PsycINFO*, as I mentioned in earlier chapters. One potentially time-saving strategy might be to locate a review article that summarizes years of research on a topic—these kinds of papers often compare the ways different researchers have measured the same thing.

CHAPTER 6

SAMPLING

In everyday life, people are free to draw inferences from a small number of incidents or observations. We don't have the time or expertise to collect large amounts of representative data, so we tend to make do with what's readily available.

Imagine a friend told you, "Nearby University is not very good. I know three people who went there, and they didn't have good experiences." In this case, your friend would be generalizing based on conversations with three students who attended a university with enrollments in the thousands. Might some students attending Nearby University have a positive view of their school? Almost certainly. Your friend's claim would be based on a sample that was not only small but haphazardly collected. What if all three students were majors in the same department—one that employed weaker teachers compared to most of the departments on campus at Nearby U? Or, what if the three students were chronic complainers who were rarely content with anything—would that cast their assertions in a new light?

Let's think about positive experiences as well. Sometimes, people ask older couples to explain the secret to a successful marriage. The assumption seems to be that anyone who has been married a long time can be considered an expert on the subject. Let's set aside the fact that the couple may not have read a single scholarly article or book on marriage (per Chapter 4). And, set aside the fact that the couple may not have developed any systematic procedures for measuring marital satisfaction or communication or other potentially relevant concepts (per Chapter 5). In this chapter, what's important to notice is that a single marriage provides a pretty limited basis from which to generalize. Two people may have been married for decades, but their relationship will differ in important ways from other marriages.

Just think about all the diverse factors that might make the experience of one marriage different from another: Some couples may be wealthy, poor, or middle-class; Christian, Muslim, Jewish, Mormon, or atheist; socially conservative or liberal; interracial or racially homogenous; dual career or single breadwinner; plagued by illness or relatively healthy; residing alone or sharing a dwelling with extended kin; surrounded by neighbors or living in an isolated rural area; and on and on this list could go. It may be flattering and cute to treat one couple's experiences as universally applicable, but it's actually a pretty weak sample from which to generalize.

Once again, my thesis in this chapter is straightforward: Researchers are better at sampling than laypersons, but their work is far from perfect.

☆ THREE REASONS RESEARCHERS USUALLY DO A BETTER JOB WITH SAMPLING

Researchers do not always have to take a sample. On rare occasions, every member of a population or all cases of a phenomenon can be studied. For example, every student in a class may be surveyed about their evaluations of an instructor, or a researcher may collect data for every known case of homicide in a particular city; in these cases, no sampling would be required as long as the data was not being used to generalize about other instructors, courses, homicides, or cities.

Most of the time, though, researchers cannot collect data so comprehensively; instead, they must study a subset of the people or incidents that interest them. Assembling that subset is called *sampling*—"the process of selecting observations . . . that will allow [researchers] to generalize to people and events not observed" (Babbie, 2010, pp. 188, 225).

There are many approaches to sampling, and I won't attempt to summarize all of them.[1] Instead, in this section, I will highlight three simple factors that make researchers better at sampling than laypersons. Then, in the subsequent section, I'll explore imperfections in scholarly sampling.

1) Researchers' samples seem, on average, larger than those collected in everyday life.

Let's revisit an article I mentioned in Chapter 3—Peyrot and Sweeney's (2000) study of the factors that shape parishioners' satisfaction with their local churches. The authors' data came from paper-and-pencil questionnaires that measured satisfaction as well as a number of variables—such as

---

[1] For a more comprehensive summary of various sampling procedures, see a conventional textbook on research methods, such as Babbie (2010, chap. 7).

the quality of the pastor, the sense of community in the congregation, and the race and gender of the parishioner—that might correlate with higher or lower satisfaction. The sample included 8,448 Catholics in 28 parishes across the metropolitan regions of Baltimore City. Questionnaires were distributed to every person who attended mass on a particular weekend and then were collected at the end of the service.

While there are weaknesses in Peyrot and Sweeney's sample (some of which I'll discuss later), there is one obvious strength: It seems pretty large in comparison to the kind of sampling that occurs in everyday life. Ordinary conversationalists, if they were especially pleased or disappointed in their church, might ask around in order to see if others agreed and why. In the parking lot or on the phone, one parishioner might ask another, "What did you think of the service today?" Such informal sampling would not likely reach anything close to the size of Peyrot and Sweeney's.

Researchers do not always collect samples that number in the thousands. Authors may perform experiments with 100 students (Simpson et al., 2011) or analyze transcripts of interviews with 56 married couples (Knudson-Martin & Mahoney, 2005) and so on. It is even possible to find articles that provide in-depth analyses of a single person, situation, or event. Persuasive arguments can be made that generalizable lessons can be drawn from very small samples if they are carefully selected (Yin, 2009).

Nevertheless, I would assert that (on average) researchers tend to collect more data from more sources than laypersons tend to do. Don't take my word for it, though. Treat size as an open question. Whenever you read an empirical journal article, imagine or observe how the topic might be "studied" in everyday life and compare the sample size with what researchers collect. (See Exercise 6.1.)

2) Researchers' samples are usually selected with more care than those collected in everyday life.

Size is not everything. More important than quantity is the quality of the samples that are collected. A large sample can be useless or even misleading if it is haphazardly collected or if its limitations are ignored.

News websites sometimes take polls of their readers and can obtain opinions from thousands of respondents. For example, in October 2012, Foxnews.com asked, "Who won the presidential debate—President Obama or Mitt Romney?" When I took the poll and viewed the results, around 95 percent (195,048) had selected Romney and 5 percent (10,259) had selected Obama. These are large numbers—more than 200,000 responses. However, the sample is not exactly carefully collected. Anyone who visits the site can vote anonymously and more than once. Readers of Foxnews.com are likely to be right leaning, but we don't even know if the responders were representative of registered Republicans because people who participate in online polls may differ in patterned ways (e.g., perhaps they are wealthier or more politically active than Republicans in general). Should we infer from the poll's results that 95 percent of those who watched the debate thought that Romney won? Should we infer that 95 percent of conservatives thought Romney won? Despite the large size of the sample, the poll's results are not much better than taking an informal vote after watching the debate at home with a few friends.

Researchers tend to put more thought into whom or what gets included in their studies. Regardless of whether their samples are bigger, they're usually better—more representative of the population about which they want to generalize or selected based on carefully conceived criteria. At the very least, researchers tend to keep track of who or what makes it into the final sample, so they can factor that into their analyses.

For example, in an impressive study of sexuality in America, Michael, Gagnon, Laumann, and Kolata (2004) carefully assembled a nationally representative sample of adults aged 18 to 59. To locate respondents, the researchers took great pains to avoid a biased sample.

> Essentially, we [chose] at random geographic areas of the country, using the equivalent of a coin toss to select them. Within those geographic regions, we randomly select[ed] cities, towns, and rural areas. Within those cities and towns we randomly select[ed] neighborhoods. Within those neighborhoods, we randomly select[ed] households. (Michael et al., 2004, p. 163; see also Laumann, Paik, & Rosen, 1999)

In the end, the researchers successfully completed more than 3,000 phone interviews. They compared the demographic characteristics of their sample with the characteristics of the population (according to the U.S. census) and found they had achieved a close match with respect to age, gender, race or ethnicity, and other variables.

Most researchers do not attempt to assemble such precisely representative samples, but they still take much care into their work. Let's recall Sun et al.'s (2003) study. Although the authors were interested in the phenomenon of binge drinking by college students, they did not attempt to sample from universities nationwide (which would be very time-consuming and expensive). Instead, they collected data at a single university in the southwestern United States—perhaps where they were employed or nearby. Within that university, Sun et al. randomly selected 120 classes and then asked instructors for permission to distribute their survey. They obtained permission to collect data in 40 classes and obtained completed questionnaires from more than 1,000 students. Although students did not sign their names, they did provide age, gender, ethnicity, year in school, place of residence (on or off campus), and other information. Again, this allowed the researchers to know what kinds of respondents were in their sample and whether it was biased in some obvious way (e.g., if males were overrepresented). Compare Sun et al.'s diligent efforts to two of the examples I discussed earlier: (1) the poll at Foxnews.com, which was filled out by "God only knows" whom, and (2) the hypothetical conversation about Nearby University that I used to start this chapter, where three haphazardly sampled students formed the basis of a confident opinion.

Large and medium-sized samples can be carefully collected, but so can very small samples. Many journal articles are based on samples of less than 100 people or cases, and they may still make important contributions to the literature. To survive peer review, authors need to explain their rationale explicitly—describing who or what is in their sample and what characteristics make it useful or generalizable. Then, reviewers and readers can agree or find flaws in the reasoning. Sociologists have long asserted that even single cases can be illuminating (Yin, 2009). Dorothy Smith (1978), for example, famously analyzed one interview (conducted by her student) in order to examine the processes by which people construct factual accounts. Her work has been reprinted and cited widely.

There is no quick rule of thumb that can be used to decide whether a sample is carefully collected or useful. More classes on research methods—and repeated exposure to journal articles—can help you figure that out.

When I read journal articles, I can almost always say to myself, "This article involves a bigger and better sample than most laypersons would collect." Try Exercise 6.1, and see what your reaction is.

Regardless of whether you agree with the choices researchers made in assembling a sample, one thing seems certain: At least the authors have empowered you to disagree. By discussing their sampling procedures, authors enable readers to understand where the data is coming from, what its weaknesses may be, and how future research might try to overcome those flaws. That is an advantage of social research in comparison to the informal and implicit sampling that occurs in everyday life.

3) Researchers (usually) tell readers who or what was included in their samples.

In the methods sections of journal articles, readers can often find clearly labeled discussions not only of researchers' sampling processes but also of their sampling outcomes. If the authors are surveying students, then what kinds of students and how many completed questionnaires? If the authors are examining newspaper coverage of a particular issue, then how many stories were included, from what newspapers, and over what time frame?

While people in everyday life can derive evidence from a range of people, observations, or experiences, they usually don't maintain a ledger documenting who or what made it into their "samples." In contrast, researchers usually do.

Sometimes authors describe the contents of their samples via an easy-to-find table. That way, readers can locate information about the sample very quickly. Sun et al. (2003) provide an example with their table titled "Characteristics of Participants." There, they list three columns of data for six variables. I'll reproduce the figures Sun et al. reported for only two of those variables—gender and class standing:

Example of a Table That Describes a Sample

	Number of respondents	Percentage of respondents
Gender		
Male	388	44.5%
Female	420	48.2%
Missing	64	7.3%
Class Standing		
Freshman	206	23.6%
Sophomore	147	16.9%
Junior	257	29.5%
Senior	262	30.0%

Source: *(adapted from Sun et al., 2003, p. 21)*

Notice how efficiently informative this table is. You can quickly look to see that all grade levels were included, though sophomores somewhat less so. You can also notice that, while there was a fairly even split of male and female respondents, quite a few people (64) chose not to answer that question.

Other scholars incorporate descriptions of their samples into regular sentences and paragraphs. This makes the information more difficult to find, but at least the information is still being provided, which is praiseworthy. For example, Peyrot and Sweeney (2000, pp. 212–213) use parenthetical comments to tell readers important details about the kinds of people who filled out questionnaires in their study.

Demographic variables include: age (seven categories; median age = 45); sex (female = 61.9 percent); race (African American = 21.2 percent, Caucasian = 70.5 percent, Other and Missing 8.3 percent) ... and marital status (Single = 27.3 percent, Married = 46.4 percent, Other and Missing = 26.3 percent).

By reporting who or what is in their samples, researchers give readers greater insight into the data that is being analyzed. After all, if a certain type of person is over- or underrepresented in a study, that might shape the results. Readers can look for potential weaknesses and then design follow-up studies intended to address those flaws. Again, compare these practices to the Foxnews.com poll I mentioned earlier as well as the hypothetical example I used to start this chapter. In both cases, you would have to guess about the characteristics of the people in those "samples" and how the distribution of those characteristics may have shaped the "findings."

I hope you'll agree that researchers usually do much better with sampling than laypersons do. Do Exercise 6.1, and see what you find.

EXERCISE 6.1

Try to find a real-life example where someone has generalized from a small, haphazardly assembled sample. Perhaps you'll notice when a friend says, "Nobody likes that movie"—an opinion that may be based on conversations your friend had with two or three people. Or, perhaps you'll notice a newscaster proclaim that there is an "epidemic" of bullying, teen pregnancies, or some other problem, based on two or three incidents that received national attention. Or, perhaps you'll hear a political pundit make a confident claim about what "all" Democrats believe or what "all" Republicans believe.

Then, try to imagine how a social scientist might sample and generalize about the same topic. Perhaps a researcher would take a larger poll or collect data from more sources. In addition to being larger, perhaps explain how a researcher's sample might be more carefully assembled; researchers might use explicit criteria for who or what should be included, and they might keep track of (and report) the characteristics of their sample.

If you are ambitious—and choose your topics carefully—then you might try to find a journal article on the same topic that you heard discussed in everyday life. You could compare the (presumably stronger) sampling procedures that were in the article to the (presumably weaker) procedures that were used by laypersons.

HOW TO FIND IMPERFECTIONS IN RESEARCHERS' SAMPLES ☆

In 2004, during the Iraq war, Secretary of Defense Donald Rumsfeld made an infamous comment: "You go to war with the army you have—not the army you might want or wish to have." Similarly, but less controversially, social scientists can usually picture an idealized sample they wish they had, as opposed to the one they do have, when they conduct their studies.

Samples are never perfect, no matter how conscientious a researcher may be. Sampling involves compromises and trade-offs. Researchers must do the best they can, given constraints of time, money, expertise, the availability and willingness of respondents, and other factors.

In this section, I'll provide three general tips that should help you critique even the most technical, statistic-laden journal article.

1) Look for authors' admissions of limitations.

Admirably, authors usually admit some of the weaknesses or drawbacks to their samples, either in the methods sections or later in the conclusion, discussion, or limitations sections of articles. Researchers should be applauded for warning readers not to overgeneralize based on their work and for identifying ways in which future researchers may improve upon what they have done. Their humility and caution is arguably another strength compared to the sampling and generalizing that occurs in everyday life.

On the other hand, admissions of limitations do provide easy evidence of imperfections in scholarly samples. For example, Sun et al. (2003) and Peyrot and Sweeney (2000) both mention limitations near the conclusions of their respective articles. These admissions are brief enough to quote in full:

> The sample of this study includes only one urban university in the Southwest— urban vs. non-urban or rural campuses might generate different findings in relation to different issues. For example, could the social norm theory be more applicable to non-urban universities? (Sun et al., 2003, p. 33)

> In considering the implications of this study one important issue is the generalizability of its findings. It is difficult to know how well the urban vicariate of Baltimore reflects the behavior and attitudes of parishioners outside the study population. (Peyrot & Sweeney, 2000, p. 219)

Here, Sun et al. (2003) admit that their sample consisted of students from only a single university. The extent and causes of binge drinking may differ for students who are not attending an urban university in the Southwest. Peyrot and Sweeney (2000), for their part, concede that their sample only comes from one metropolitan area on the East Coast, which may differ from other regions in important ways. Both articles humbly admit flaws in their sampling.

2) Build on the authors' admissions of limitations.

As we have just seen, authors' confessions of weakness can be fairly brief. Researchers may admit problems with their samples but do so in a minimalist fashion. Thus, to develop a more robust critique, you might elaborate on the authors' admissions or find additional areas of weakness that the authors neglect to mention.

Consider Sun et al. (2003). They concede that they only sampled students from a university in the Southwest. So, a critic could elaborate on that limitation by raising questions regarding whether drinking patterns (and causes) might vary among students who live on the East Coast, the South, the Midwest, or in remote regions like Alaska or Hawaii. Might binge drinking be influenced by regional differences in culture, weather, recreational options, and so on? Or, could different regions attract particular kinds of students, who bring with them different kinds of drinking beliefs and practices?

Next, you could consider closely related factors that Sun et al. (2003) neglected to mention. For example, the authors don't say whether the university was a public or private institution or whether the school was known for its prominent sports teams. Might private school students drink at different rates, and for different reasons, than public school students? Might the presence of popular football or basketball programs shape students' binge drinking to some degree? Perhaps private school students have more discretionary income or more conservative attitudes, or perhaps athletically oriented universities attract and encourage more binge drinkers.

Thus, by fleshing out researchers' admissions of limitations, it is possible to develop a fuller and more vigorous critique of their samples.

3) Look for any other ways that the sample may be significantly different than the population that researchers want to generalize about.

The population that Sun et al. (2003) were interested in generalizing about—as stated in their paper's title and literature review—was "college students." Thus, to launch our critiques in Points 1 and 2, we simply thought about the potentially important ways that college students vary and considered whether these variations were represented in the authors' sample.

The same strategy can be applied to many studies. Any study can be criticized if the characteristics of its sample differ (in potentially significant ways) from the characteristics of the population to which the researchers want to generalize.

The more broadly generalizable researchers want their studies to be, the easier it is to critique their work. Many social scientists study fundamental dimensions of the human experience; consequently, they state or imply that their work is applicable to humanity in general. In studies of decision making, motivation, human development, close relationships, and other topics, researchers often suggest (implicitly or explicitly) that their analyses could be applicable to people everywhere. Recall that Peyrot and Sweeney (2000) wrote about "parishioners [in general]" and Sun et al. (2003) wrote about "college students [in general]." These authors did not specify that their studies were relevant to American parishioners or to college students in the United States.

Americans constitute only about 5 percent of the world population. They are among the weirdest people in the world—WEIRD because they live in a Western, educated, industrialized, rich, and democratic society (Henrich, Heine, & Norenzayan, 2010). The other 95 percent of the planet may sometimes think, feel, and behave very differently than Americans do, especially those who live in less-educated, less-industrialized, less-wealthy, and less-democratic societies. Might people in the Dominican Republic relate to their parishes differently than people in Baltimore do? Might college students in India binge drink at different rates and for different reasons than students in the Southwest United States?

American college students might further be described as the WEIRDest of the WEIRD because they tend to come from more-educated and wealthy families within the United States (Henrich et al., 2010). Yet, many researchers—in psychology, sociology, education, and other disciplines—often rely on undergraduates for data because of the ease of access. Need data? Why not use your students! Students are easily found, and they are often eager to participate in research as it can provide a legitimate learning opportunity. (Also, keep in mind that participation may be factored into students' course grades in the form of extra credit.)

Arnett (2008) humorously proposed that the *Journal of Personality and Social Psychology (JPSP)* be renamed the *Journal of the Personality and Social Psychology of American Undergraduate Introductory Psychology Students* in order to more accurately reflect the composition of the samples that appear in that outlet. Arnett (2008, p. 604) found that, in the year 2007, 67 percent of *JPSP* articles published by American authors relied on samples consisting of undergraduate psychology students. Moreover, these students were usually attending major research universities rather than community colleges and other institutions of higher education.

Thus, a sample that is intended to be generalizable to people everywhere can be criticized for being too WEIRD if it consists only of Americans or American college students. This is simply another manifestation of the trick we used in Subsections 1 and 2 above. In each of the three parts of this section, we have simply tried to look for significant ways that a sample may differ from the population that researchers want to generalize about.

This strategy is not the only way to critique a sample. But, it does provide a relatively reliable place to start.

EXERCISE 6.2

Find and read an empirical journal article that interests you; it might be a paper that you used in Chapters 3, 4, or 5.

Notice who or what made it into the sample. Also, try to figure out whether the researchers are generalizing to a particular population. Do they suggest that their findings are relevant to college students, or to Americans, or to humanity in general, or what?

To begin the fun part—your critique—just start with what the authors tell you. Do the authors describe any drawbacks to their sample? These admissions could be mentioned in the methods section, or near the conclusion of the article, or even in a footnote.

Next, try to elaborate on the authors' admitted limitations. Could you give a more detailed explanation of a particular flaw that the authors mention?

Lastly, can you identify other potential flaws that the authors fail to admit? What are some potentially important ways that the authors' sample may diverge from the population that they want to generalize about?

CONCLUSION ☆

This chapter began by making positive comparisons between scholarly samples and those collected by laypersons. In everyday life, people are free to generalize based on information they collected from just a few haphazard observations. In contrast, researchers do better. Social scientists try to collect larger samples more carefully—often using explicit and thoughtful criteria to assemble their samples. Researchers tell their readers about the procedures they used to collect their samples as well as the outcomes of their efforts—who or what went into the samples.

Researchers deserve our applause and respect for their efforts. Nevertheless, their work can also be approached with a healthy degree of skepticism. No sample is perfect. In the face of a variety of constraints, researchers collect useful yet flawed samples. Authors themselves usually admit their samples' limitations—or at least some of the limitations—briefly.

Even a newcomer to social science can develop a fairly elaborate critique of a researcher's sampling strategies. To do so, a critical reader can start with the author's admitted limitations and then elaborate on those. Ask yourself, Does the sample differ in significant ways from the population to which the authors want to generalize?

CHAPTER 7

ANALYSIS

As a sophomore in college, I shared an apartment with three friends I met in the dorms. One of them—"Jeremy"—had grown up in an extremely wealthy family. Jeremy was a humorous and affable guy, but after a few weeks of living together, I noticed that he tended to leave his dirty dishes scattered around the apartment. Mostly eaten bowls of cereal were abandoned in front of the television or on the kitchen table—as if Jeremy's meal had been interrupted by some emergency ("Gotta go-go-go!"). Loading the dishwasher or scrubbing a pan seemed completely foreign to him.

"Jeremy never does the dishes!" I complained to my other two apartment mates.

"Yeah, what's up with that?"

"Probably he was spoiled as a kid. I bet his family had a full-time maid!"

Then my two roommates and I devised a plan to give Jeremy some gentle reminders, which produced mixed results, but that's a long story.

This mundane example may sound remote from social science, but there are some familiar and researchable questions in play: Who's doing what? How frequently is a phenomenon occurring, and why?

In everyday life, we raise these sorts of questions more often than we may realize. We routinely collect data, analyze it, and present our findings to others. In the example above, my roommates and I had engaged in some casual observations of Jeremy's behavior and formulated an explanation. Was it accurate to assert that Jeremy "never" cleaned any dishes? Probably not. Were there other factors that might explain his neglect of the dishes? Probably so. Our data collection, analysis, and findings were pretty shoddy.

My roommates and I could have behaved more "sciency" if we had carefully observed Jeremy's behavior over the course of several weeks, measured the number of dishes he cleaned versus the number he left dirty, calculated a precise frequency (e.g., "Jeremy cleans up after himself 37 percent of the time"), and investigated a wider range of variables[1] that might explain his behavior—such as his busy work, school, and fraternity schedule, relationship dysfunctions within the apartment, different standards of cleanliness, cultural notions of dishwashing as "feminine," and so on.

Needless to say, we did not do any of that. It would seem odd—if not morally repugnant—to subject a roommate to such scrutiny. Yet, laypersons' reticence to conduct rigorous inquiries into everyday life is not shared by social scientists. Researchers want to know—as best they can—what's happening, how often, and why. That strong drive to know helps make social science better than ordinary human inquiry.

☆ THE ANALYTICAL STRENGTHS OF SOCIAL RESEARCH

As with conceptualization, literature reviews, measurement, and sampling, researchers' efforts are superior to laypersons' when it comes to analyzing and presenting data. Rather than jumping to conclusions based on a few haphazardly collected pieces of information, social scientists tend to search for more data, and then they systematically search through that data to find subtle patterns. I guess there's a reason why they're called *re-searchers*. Social scientists look, and look again, for information that might confirm or contradict their theories and expectations.

Let's briefly discuss researchers' analytical strengths before we turn to weaknesses.

1) Social scientists carefully scrutinize their data using sophisticated analytical techniques, and they report their findings precisely and cautiously.

Social scientists have developed a wide range of impressive analytical techniques, both quantitative and qualitative. On the quantitative side, statistical software packages (such as SPSS) enable researchers to analyze thousands of pieces of data simultaneously. Qualitative researchers, too, can use computer software to code hundreds or thousands of pages of interview transcripts and field notes. And, even when no sophisticated technology is

---

[1] In journal articles, the term *variable* is often used instead of *concept* in order to highlight the fact that a phenomenon varies—it can be present or not present, or (in some cases) there can be more or less of it. In the previous section of this chapter, I mentioned the issues of temperature, binge drinking, and intelligence—these could be considered variables in a study. They can be measured and correlated: Do more people engage in binge drinking when the temperature is higher? Is binge drinking associated with a lower level of intelligence?

employed, researchers bring a great deal of expertise, determination, and concentration to the data they analyze.

As quantitative articles are the main focus of this book, let's elaborate on that form of analysis. Researchers who use statistical software can examine thousands of pieces of data—more than any one person could possibly hold in his or her head at once (and far more than the five or ten observations that my friends and I made of Jeremy's behavior). Quantitative researchers can look for correlations among numerous variables in ways that far surpass ordinary human capabilities.

Two variables are positively correlated when an increase in one variable is associated with as increase in the other; for example, perhaps the variable of dishwashing goes up the more people feel connected to their apartment mates. A negative correlation is when an increase in one variable leads to a decrease in another variable; perhaps the more hours a person is employed outside the home, the less time they spend doing dishes.

Social scientists can search for positive and negative correlations across hundreds or thousands of cases—and they can do so for many variables simultaneously, not just two variables. They usually report these correlations, along with other important statistics, in clearly marked tables. Compare this to everyday life, where people (1) routinely use hyperbolic phrases (e.g., "You always . . ." or "He never . . .") and (2) fixate on one causal variable (e.g., childhood upbringing). In journal articles, researchers tend to be more cautious, thorough, and precise in reporting their findings. They specify that exact degree to which one variable is correlated with other variables, and they use tentative phrases such as "Childhood experiences with housework appear to be an important factor" rather than speaking in terms of absolutes.

In sections on results, discussion, and conclusions, scholars draw connections between their findings and the results of earlier studies, noting any consistencies or contradictions. Authors invite future researchers to conduct additional studies that might corroborate or challenge their results. Though an article may take many months or even years to write, scholars usually remain humble about their findings and admit the limitations of their studies.

I would argue that this reporting style is far superior to confidence with which laypersons declare impromptu "truths" based on quick and haphazard data collection and analysis. Don't take my word for it. Do Exercise 7.1, and see for yourself.

2) Social scientists base their analyses on theoretical arguments about the constraints that shape human behavior.

In everyday life, we are free to make confident arguments based on the first theory that comes to mind. If a roommate isn't doing the dishes, then maybe it's due to his wealthy childhood—sure, good enough. Anything that sounds plausible may suffice, and there is no requirement that we read or think deeply about other possible factors.

In contrast, and as we discussed in Chapter 3, social scientists perform extensive literature reviews in conjunction with their research. From this reading, they are exposed to a wide range of theoretical perspectives and causal arguments. Moreover, editors and peer reviewers often ask scholars to consider factors that they may have left out of the first draft of the articles they submit for possible publication. As a result of this thinking, social scientists tend to have more nuanced, complicated, and wide-ranging explanations for human behavior.

Theoretical explanations vary somewhat by discipline (e.g., brain chemistry is more relevant in psychology than sociology) and also within disciplines (as there many different kinds of psychologists, many of whom don't study the brain at all). Yet, despite the theoretical diversity, there are overlapping concerns. In journal articles—especially quantitative ones—the emphasis is usually on *constraints,* or factors that shape behavior. Let's pause to explore the notion of constraints by relating it to a simple example: the food you eat.

Some scholars examine the biological constraints that shape conduct—such as the ways our bodies and brains may be "hardwired" to seek out fats, sugar, and salt or how some people may have a predisposition to alcoholism. Other scholars focus on geographical constraints—such as the kinds of crops that can be grown, given the local climate and soil. Probably the majority of social scientists, however, tend to emphasize either external social constraints or internal social constraints (see Berger, 1963).

External social constraints are those social forces that surround us and guide our behavior. Picture a maze or a prison—there may be directions you want to go, but there are obstacles in your way. With respect to the food you eat, we might say that your choices are guided by many external factors:

- What kinds of food are offered in stores or restaurants in your area? If they don't sell it (e.g., red bananas, okra, sushi, etc.), then you probably won't eat it.
- How expensive is the food that surrounds you? If fresh vegetables are more expensive than processed foods, that might shape your choices.
- What are the general food norms in your particular region? In some countries (but not others), it is acceptable to eat cows, dogs, worms, deer penises, bull testicles, and duck embryos. Will you be encouraged or rewarded for eating certain foods, or will you be criticized or ostracized?
- Do the food norms vary by age, gender, race, class, and other variables? A small jar of baby food might be tasty and convenient, but an American teenager who ate it for lunch would risk being ridiculed. Similarly, sometimes men may be disparaged for drinking "feminine" drinks (e.g., appletinis, wine coolers), while women may be discouraged from ordering "manly" drinks (e.g., whiskey, dark beer); as a result, they might avoid such beverages even if they like the taste.

Internal social constraints are those forces that guide our conduct because we internalize them. Picture a robot that is programmed to think and do certain things. People are taught certain beliefs, perspectives, and identities. We often learn to want that which our culture or subculture has encouraged us to want. For example:

- You may be taught to believe that cows are sacred and off-limits (rather than a routine source of hamburgers) or that lobster is a delicacy (rather than a large, underwater bug). Hence, what you want to make for dinner will be shaped by these beliefs, even if you are eating alone with nobody watching.
- Your college friends may persuade you that eating meat is immoral and unhealthy. These beliefs might then shape your conduct and your emotions whenever your parents serve up a big Thanksgiving turkey or holiday ham.
- Through exposure to messages in mass media, you may be encouraged to acquire a positive identity—such as "I am a slender person, not fat" or "I am muscular and strong, not weak"—which may shape how many calories you consume or how much protein you eat.

In my discussion of four types of constraints, I have avoided technical terms and complicated theories in order to make a simple point: Social scientists consider and explore a range of factors when they study human behavior. They are aware that anything we do can be shaped by numerous forces from many different directions. They read the existing literature to determine what those forces may be and what effect previous studies have found them to have. They use this theoretical knowledge before, as, and after they analyze their data.

When I read empirical journal articles, I almost always come away with the feeling that the researchers have attempted to bring more theoretical awareness and sophistication than laypersons would bring to the same topic. Don't take my word for it, though. Do Exercise 7.1—repeatedly, if you can—and see for yourself.

EXERCISE 7.1

1. **Search for an example of "data analysis" in your everyday life.** You might focus on a discussion of why some person is engaging in a particular behavior (besides dishwashing, as I covered that topic). Listen to what you and your friends say in ordinary conversations, or to what politicians and pundits say on television, or to what your coaches, parents, priests, coworkers, or employers say.

(Continued)

(Continued)

2. **Can you identify the weaknesses of this everyday analysis like I did with the case of Jeremy?** You might describe a better way of analyzing data and reporting findings about the topic—one that is more scientific. Can you think of some factors or social constraints that were neglected in the discussion?

3. **If you are ambitious, try to find a journal article on a topic similar to the discussion you examined in #1.** Search the methods and analysis sections of the journal article. Find and (as best you can) describe the type of analysis that the researchers used and the variables or factors they included in their study. Identify examples of precision and cautiousness in the text or in the tables the authors provide. Can you explain why the researchers' efforts are more impressive than the discussion you heard in the everyday example you found in #1 above?

☆ FINDING ANALYTICAL WEAKNESSES IN SOCIAL RESEARCH

Social scientists' analytical skills far surpass those that are usually employed in ordinary human inquiry. Nevertheless, researchers are far from perfect. In this section, I will discuss two simple strategies for critiquing the kinds of analyses that regularly appear in standard journal articles (SJAs).

1) Whenever researchers perform an analysis, they must be selective about the factors or variables they include.

Researchers do the best they can to take into account as many of the factors that existing theories and previous research suggest are important. However, no scholar can focus on everything. Very few journal articles consider external constraints, internal constraints, biological constraints, and geographical constraints all at the same time. And even if a scholar focuses on a particular form of constraint—such as external factors—they can't include everything that falls under that category. Instead, scholars tend to have *pet theories* and *pet variables*—forms of explanation that they prefer and hope to support. Rather than fully exploring every possible perspective and every possible factor that relates to their topic, they tend to craft research projects that revolve around particular orientations and issues. If they find evidence that supports their preferred theory and causal factors—or discredits a competing orientation—then so much the better.

As a result of these predilections, the literature that scholars read and summarize tends to be somewhat delimited rather than expansive and inclusive. Researchers do not have time, nor do journals offer the space, for truly comprehensive literature reviews—as we saw in Chapter 4.

Moreover, a further winnowing down of scholars' analytical focus occurs when authors move from their literature reviews to their methodology sections. Researchers face limitations in the data they can collect. Some information may simply not be accessible or affordable, which complicates the tasks of sampling and measurement. Consequently, most researchers cannot truly test every theoretical notion they might want to; their data can only speak to a portion of the theoretical ideas they would like to apply to their topic.

Recall Sun et al.'s (2003) study of binge drinking by college students. A wide range of factors might influence whether a person tends to drink excessively. Although Sun et al. conducted admirable research, they cannot account for every potentially important factor. In their analysis, the authors included only 13 variables. The selection of these was shaped by the authors' reading of the literature as well as by the questionnaire that they adopted— a document that was created by prior researchers. Let's look through these variables and, as you read them, imagine whether each one might have some influence on whether or not you engaged in binge drinking:

1) Gender of respondent

2) Age of respondent

3) Ethnic origin of respondent

4) Marital status of respondent

5) Respondent's living arrangements—e.g., living with parents, living with spouse, living with roommates, living alone

6) Family history of alcohol or drug use (e.g., by a parent or sibling)

7) Precollege history of alcohol use by respondent

8) Whether respondent's close friends disapprove of binge drinking

9) Whether respondent believes that alcohol has positive effects (e.g., allows people to have more fun)

10) Whether respondent believes that binge drinking brings great risk, some risk, or no risk

11) Whether respondent has experienced peer pressure to binge drink

12) Whether respondent believes that drinking is central part of social life on campus

13) What respondent believes about alcohol use by "the average student" on campus

There are some important and logical variables being studied here. It seems clear that the decision to binge drink could (in some cases) be shaped by each factor. Sun et al. (2003) should be applauded for attempting to determine if there was a positive or negative correlation between these variables and the practice of binge drinking.

Nevertheless, this list of 13 variables is far from exhaustive. Despite the time and effort that Sun et al. (2003) put into their research, they ended up neglecting a wide range of potentially relevant factors. I'll list some below:

1) Whether respondent has a physiological proclivity to binge drink

2) Respondent's religious beliefs

3) Respondent's socioeconomic status (e.g., personal income, parents' household income)

4) Whether respondent works full time, part time, or not at all

5) Whether respondent is a member of a fraternity or sorority

6) Respondent's major

7) Whether respondent attends a university that is officially *dry* (i.e., no alcohol allowed)

8) The number and proximity of local stores that sell alcohol

9) Whether respondent is living in a location where taxes on liquor are much higher or lower than the national average

10) Respondent's exposure to advertisements, television shows, and movies that promote alcohol consumption

Arguably, all ten of these factors could have some influence on whether a person tends to drink excessively. Some of these issues—#3 and #6—were included on the questionnaire that Sun et al. (2003) used, yet (for potentially good reasons) the researchers chose not to incorporate them into their analysis. Some of these issues are admittedly more difficult to measure—such as #10. Moreover, some issues seem beyond the scope of what a social scientist might be expected to study—#1 is arguably a topic for biologists (e.g., Herman, Philbeck, Vasilopoulos, & Depetrillo, 2003). But, none of that matters. If you can imagine a potentially important factor that might increase or decrease a person's likelihood of binge drinking, then you can legitimately argue that Sun et al.'s (2003) work is imperfect for ignoring that factor.

Perfection is a high standard. Most authors wouldn't take offense at the critique of selectivity because they recognize (more than laypersons do) just how complicated social life is. As long as readers recognize that a study is better than ordinary human inquiry and admit that the authors' work is useful (or is at least a serious attempt to conduct a careful study), then the charge of selective analysis is welcomed by most researchers. Such discussions can even be enjoyable and can provoke ideas for future research. In their articles' conclusions, authors sometimes call attention to (some of the) factors or forces that they neglected in order to prompt future researchers to address those limitations in follow-up studies.

Test your ability to identify selectivity in the analyses that appear in journal articles by doing Exercise 7.2.

EXERCISE 7.2

Read a journal article that interests you—perhaps a paper that you used for the exercises in Chapters 3 through 6. Look in the methods section and find the variables that the authors include in their analysis. Then, think of at least two variables that the researchers could have studied but didn't. Try to explain why these factors are potentially important. If possible, discuss at least one internal social constraint and one external social constraint.

---

2) Causal order

A second way to critique a journal article is to challenge authors' assumptions about the causal relationships that exist between the variables they study. For example, in Sun et al.'s (2003) analysis, the dependent variable was whether or not respondents engaged in binge drinking. There were 13 independent variables in the study, including "Whether respondent's close friends disapprove of binge drinking." Sun et al. crunched the numbers and found that this independent variable ("close friends disapproval") had a strong negative correlation with the dependent variable ("binge drinking"). As disapproval increased, binge drinking tended to decrease.[2]

This makes intuitive sense: It is easy to imagine that our close friends might exert a strong influence over our drinking behavior. Let's refer to this causal influence as X→Y.

On the other hand, it is also easy to imagine an alternative scenario: Perhaps students who are already predisposed to binge drinking tend to seek out companions who engage in that practice. If I want to "party hard," maybe I will tend to form close friendships with people who

---

[2] Respondents who indicated that their close friends did "not disapprove" of binge drinking were 4.54 times more likely to engage in that practice than respondents who said their close friends would "strongly disapprove" (Sun et al., 2003, p. 23).

are likeminded. In this scenario, Y→X. An inclination to binge drink shapes the kinds of friends we have.

So, which is it? Does X→Y, or does Y→X, or both? It makes a difference. If researchers want to understand why a phenomenon is occurring, then they need to unravel the complexities of causal order. (I'm tempted to call this the *chicken-egg dilemma*.) Otherwise, we get some funny-looking sentences like this: The independent variable may depend on the dependent variable.

One way researchers attempt to deal with this dilemma is to conduct longitudinal research. By collecting data over time, social scientists can sometimes show that changes in one variable precede changes in another variable. So, we might notice patterns where students' drinking practices change after they form close friendships with people who approve or disapprove of excessive alcohol consumption.

Unfortunately, longitudinal research is comparatively rare. It is more expensive and difficult to conduct and still provides no guarantee that a researcher will be able to unravel causal order dilemmas. Most research is *cross-sectional*—collecting data at one point in time—so researchers must make larger assumptions and inferences about causal order.

Thus, an effective strategy for critiquing many (but not all) journal articles is to look for problems with causal order, as we did with the example of binge drinking. My undergraduate students have successfully used this strategy to highlight imperfections in articles on a wide range of topics—even research that employs statistically sophisticated forms of analysis. Below are some examples. I'll include (X) and (Y) in order to help you find the causal order dilemmas:

- Wong (1997) studied some of the factors that shaped whether Canadian youth of Chinese decent would engage in delinquent acts. He hypothesized that adherence to Chinese culture (X) may lower delinquency (Y) due to that culture's emphasis on family commitment and moral values. However, one can ask whether engaging in delinquency (Y) may lead to a rejection of Chinese culture (X) due to the resocialization that can occur during interactions with fellow delinquents.
- Peyrot and Sweeney (2000, p. 219) examined whether parishioners' satisfaction with their pastor's performance (X) shaped their overall satisfaction with their local church (Y). But, the authors admit that parishioners' global sense of satisfaction (Y) may shape the satisfaction they feel with specific dimensions of their church, including the pastor's performance (X). Perhaps you've heard of the halo effect?
- Brandl, Stroshine, and Frank (2001, p. 527) noted that police officers who make more arrests tend to receive more complaints about excessive force. However, they could not say unequivocally if arrests (X) led to complaints about excessive force (Y) or if excessive force was used (Y) and then arrests were made in an attempt to justify it or cover it up (X).

- Klendauer and Deller (2009) investigated whether perceptions of unfairness (X) led people to feel less committed to the companies they work for (Y). However, they admitted that people who feel less committed (Y) may be more inclined to perceive situations as unfair (X) compared to people who feel more committed.
- Simpson et al. (2011) set out to study whether "feeling powerful" (X) improves people's memories of social networks (Y). But, one might ask whether having a good memory (Y) may be helpful in obtaining power or feeling powerful (X).

These examples are not meant to be representative of all social science; they are merely some simple examples intended to demonstrate how to make a causal order argument. Causal order may or may not be an issue in the journal articles you read. Try Exercise 7.3, with a few articles on different topics, and see what you find.

EXERCISE 7.3

Skim through a quantitative journal article that interests you. Pay extra attention to the description of the variables in the methods section, so you can quickly identify the authors' independent and dependent variables. Don't stop there, though. The literature review and any discussion or limitations sections may prove helpful.

Can you explain and then critique the authors' assumptions about the causal order of their independent and dependent variables? Can you argue that it is just as likely—or at least somewhat likely—that the dependent variable could have a causal effect on one of the independent variables?

Unlike Exercise 7.2, I cannot guarantee that this line of questioning will always generate results. Many articles exhibit trouble with causal order, but some don't. You may need your instructor to help you find a workable article in order to complete this exercise.

CONCLUSION ☆

In everyday life, a few casual observations provide enough data to declare that a trend is taking place and to speculate about its supposed causes. After a few unfortunate incidents, a journalist or pundit may state, "There is an 'epidemic' of school shootings—is bullying to blame?" Or, college roommates may decide, "Jeremy never does the dishes. He must have been spoiled as a child."

In contrast, social scientists usually collect more data more carefully, and they look for trends and patterns using rigorous analytical techniques.

Research often involves hundreds or thousands of pieces of data. Information can be compiled for many different variables, and computer programs can be used to model the relationships between them. From their reading of prior studies, social scientists bring a deeper theoretical understanding of the many constraints that shape human behavior, which informs their sampling, measurements, and analyses. Then, as they compose their final reports, researchers describe their findings with precision and caution rather than speaking in hyperbole. All of this is, arguably, far superior to ordinary human inquiry.

Yet, research is far from perfect. Researchers can't help but neglect potentially relevant factors as they collect and analyze their data. Virtually any study can be criticized for what it left out—due to the researchers' theoretical preferences, due to methodological constraints, or due to simple human error. When researchers investigate what is going on and why, they unavoidably ignore some important causal forces as they focus on what is most interesting, and study-able, for them.

Moreover, researchers may speak of independent and dependent variables (X→Y), but trouble with causal order is often present, with the latter variable potentially influencing the former (Y→X). Studies can often be criticized for treating as an independent variable a phenomenon that may actually be shaped by (or dependent on) the dependent variable. If the goal of the research is to illuminate the intricacies of what causes what, then an article can be reasonably criticized for any problematic causal order assumptions that haunt the analysis. Admirably, social scientists often admit when such dilemmas exist, which makes the job of critical thinking—finding imperfections in research while appreciating its strengths—a bit easier.

CHAPTER **8**

ETHICS

In Chapters 8 and 9, we'll focus on two moral issues that are relevant to almost any empirical journal article—ethics and politics. These two concepts are, of course,[1] complex and difficult to define. For the purposes of this book, *ethics* has to do with the morality of research practices: Do researchers treat respondents fairly and humanely, or are they doing harm to those who participate in their studies? *Politics* has to do with the morality of research goals or purposes: What positive or negative consequences will the research have on the world? How might a study's findings be used to further some moral agenda beyond the halls of academia?

This chapter focuses on ethics. Compared to the explicit attention that researchers tend to give to their conceptual definitions, literature reviews, measurements, sampling, and analytical techniques, ethics can sometimes be given short shrift. Nevertheless, important ethical questions can be asked of most studies, and comparisons can be made with the more casual investigations that people undertake in their everyday lives.

ETHICS IN EVERYDAY LIFE: CASUAL SNOOPING AND GOSSIP ☆

My wife and I don't have children, though we've been married for almost 15 years. Over that time, many friends, relatives, and acquaintances have asked, "Do you have any kids?" and "When are you going to have kids?" When we reply that we aren't going to have children, they often appear somewhat surprised and ask, "Really? Why not?"

---

[1] See Chapter 3 on conceptualization.

In the course of a sociable conversation, these questions appear quite ordinary and routine. Even to me they seem mildly amusing—"At least we're not talking about the weather," I tell myself. My spouse also seems to take the questioning in stride, for the most part.

Yet, if you think about it, such questioning is fraught with peril. Simple questions about having children could generate quite a bit of embarrassment, shame, sadness, and even distress. What if my spouse and I have fertility issues or sexual dysfunction? Or, maybe we lost our first child in a devastating tragedy and can't bring ourselves to try again. Perhaps we doubt our ability to adequately parent due to financial reasons (we could have large student loans, medical expenses, etc.) or due to emotional reasons (we could be in marital counseling on the verge of divorce). Maybe a genetic illness runs in our families, causing some trepidation about raising an afflicted child. Or, perhaps we have fervent beliefs about the destructive environmental effects of overpopulation. Maybe we also realize that discussing any of these issues could expose us to unwanted pity or to ridicule.[2]

Along with risky questioning, everyday conversationalists also engage in snooping and gossiping. Friends, neighbors, and other companions want to know: who is having relationship trouble, who is having financial success, who has gained or lost weight, who votes Democratic or Republican, and so on. People look and listen to discover the latest, and then they reveal and discuss it with others. "Guess what! I found out why the Joneses don't have kids," you might imagine someone saying. With the advent of the Internet, personal information obtained by snooping or gossip can now be shared by text, chat, and e-mail, or posted on a website, leading to the public disparagement of someone's reputation. (One of the most notorious cases involves an undergraduate at Rutgers who used a hidden camera to display his roommate's sexual encounter on the web.)

I'm painting a grim picture. It's also true that people can be tactful— they're sometimes cautious about asking sensitive questions, minding their own business, and keeping secrets to themselves.

Nonetheless, I would argue that, on average, social scientists tend to do a better job of collecting and sharing information in an ethical manner—as I hope to show in the next section.

---

[2]Actually, the ridicule has happened. My niece and sister-in-law have both (separately) informed me that people who don't have children are "weird." Per Chapter 3, I'm sure they carefully read the literature on child-free couples (Park, 2005; Agrillo & Nelini, 2008) before they formed their confident opinions, right? Nah, of course not.

ETHICAL PRACTICES THAT SET SOCIAL RESEARCH
ABOVE ORDINARY HUMAN INQUIRY ☆

Like everyday conversationalists, social scientists are often very interested in people's private lives. Researchers ask detailed questions about highly personal topics, from less risky inquiries—such as "Who will you vote for in the upcoming presidential election?" and "How many hours of television do you watch each week?"—to highly sensitive inquiries—such as "Have you ever had a venereal disease?" and "How often do you have suicidal thoughts?"

Researchers store this information for months or years, and share it with others, by making presentations at conferences and publishing articles in journals. Yet, they rarely cause anyone any public embarrassment or engage in anything that resembles ordinary gossip.

Researchers employ a number of practices that make their investigations much more ethically sound than the casual inquiries that people conduct in everyday life. Social scientists take numerous steps to avoid harming those who participate in their studies.

First, before making contact with respondents, researchers usually think through the ethical dilemmas they may face. For example, survey researchers will carefully read and reread the questions they plan to ask respondents and imagine how each item might be interpreted or received by respondents. They adjust phrasing so that it is less likely to make respondents feel threatened; they adjust the order of the questions in order to ease into more sensitive topics. Ordinary conversationalists may engage in some of these behaviors as well (so as not to offend their companions) but (most likely) not with the amount of forethought and planning that researchers exhibit.

Also, before research begins, social scientists regularly submit their research proposals to an institutional review board (IRB), which usually consists of university faculty and staff. IRBs double-check that researchers are not engaging in potentially harmful conduct and encourage researchers to imagine and prepare for what could go wrong. Moreover, scholars often receive informal feedback on their research plans from collaborators and mentors. And, as part of their literature reviews, researchers read about the ethical dilemmas that prior scholars have encountered and the strategies that can be used to deal with them. In addition, the scholarly associations that researchers join—such as the American Sociological Association (ASA) and American Psychological Association (APA)[3]—have ethical codes of conduct that members must agree to abide by.

---

[3] See http://www.apa.org/ethics/code/index.aspx and http://www.asanet.org/about/ethics.cfm.

Researchers usually obtain informed consent from research participants with whom they interact. Subjects are told that their participation is voluntary and that they may cease participation at any time without retribution. A respondent can hang up during a phone survey, rip up his or her paper-and-pencil questionnaire, walk out of an experiment, and so on, without fear of reprisal. Researchers usually seek confirmation (verbally or in writing) that subjects understand the voluntary nature of their participation before a study proceeds. In contrast, imagine how a similar situation may play out in everyday life: If we dislike a line of questioning, we may say, "None of your business," and walk away, but that will likely generate negative emotions and damage personal relationships among our coworkers, friends, and family—people whom we may see on a regular basis.

Earlier I stated that ordinary conversationalists seem to have much curiosity and long memories for gossip. Social scientists, too, want to collect and store personal information, but they take steps to ensure that information does not leak out and harm anyone's reputation—or their relationships, employment prospects, self-esteem, and so on. Researchers sometimes keep data under lock and key or on hard drives that are password protected or not networked. They may separate the data from the name of the person who supplied it so that no one—in some studies not even the researchers themselves—can connect a particular set of answers with any particular individual.

Perhaps most importantly, researchers almost never publicly reveal the identities of respondents. In the case of statistical data, responses are grouped so that no participant is identifiable. If the data is qualitative, social scientists tend to protect the source. For example, if a respondent is quoted at length, then the researcher will withhold or change the name of the speaker; moreover, any personally identifying information within the quote may be deleted or altered so that readers cannot connect any particular statement with any specific individual.

Ethical Dilemmas

Social scientists tend to behave cautiously when they collect data and publish their findings. Nevertheless, they're not perfect. On very rare occasions, scholars make stunningly immoral choices. But what's more interesting are the common ethical gray areas that pervade social research. Even the most well-intentioned researchers face ethical dilemmas that defy simple solutions and snap judgments. Different courses of action can each have pros and cons that must be identified and compared. A researcher's conduct may be morally praiseworthy from one point of view but reprehensible from another.

Consider the following examples, which by no means constitute an exhaustive or representative list. I have focused on only one area of research ethics—that of informed consent—in order to provide some illustrations of the kinds of ethical dilemmas that pervade social research.

• Researchers are not supposed to coerce people into participating in their studies. Participation should be voluntary. Yet, when a professor asks students to fill out a survey or partake in an experiment, do respondents feel any pressure to oblige? Do students wonder if their grades will be impacted by nonparticipation (Babbie, 2010, p. 65)? Participation may be described as optional because it is merely a chance to earn extra credit, but if the students are graded on a curve, then is it truly optional? To resolve this dilemma, students may be offered an alternative way to obtain extra credit. But if the alternative—such as writing a paper—is perceived as onerous, then is a subtle form of coercion still taking place? (See Trafimow, Madson, & Gwizdowski, 2006, p. 247)

• Before collecting data from an organization, a researcher may (quite appropriately) seek permission from someone in a position of authority. Once obtained, the researcher may then proceed to obtain informed consent from subordinates in that organization. However, might those subordinates' participation be influenced by the implicit or explicit endorsement of their superiors? For example, if a CEO allows a researcher to collect data about his or her company, then might the workers feel pressure (real or imagined) to participate?

• When collecting data from children, an IRB may require researchers to obtain informed consent from parents or legal guardians. This seems sensible as children are a vulnerable population that must be given extra protection. However, the requirement adds a layer of difficulty and creates new ethical dilemmas. For example, parents may not be aware that their children engage in certain behaviors, such as smoking, sexual intercourse, or gang activity. Should researchers inform parents that their children have been selected for inclusion in a study because of these behaviors? What punitive harm might befall the children? Or, alternatively, what benefits may come to the children? (Diviak, Curry, Emery, & Mermelstein, 2004; Israel & Hay, 2006, p. 72)

• Should small financial incentives be used to entice low-income people to participate in research? Is that a way of exploiting the poor, or would not offering compensation be exploitive? (Israel & Hay, 2006, p. 65)

• The goal of obtaining informed consent is important, but so is the goal of obtaining accurate information. At times, the two goals seem in conflict. Some researchers argue that consent forms can bias their samples (as some people refuse to participate when presented with a legalistic document) and their data (as some people may behave differently after signing such documents). Researchers often chafe when an IRB requires usage of a long informed-consent document. (Israel & Hay, 2006, pp. 66-68)

• The success of many experiments depends on participants not knowing what the point of the study is. Should researchers compensate for this deception by debriefing participants at the end of the study? Will understanding the point of a study make participants feel better or worse about being deceived? (Babbie, 2010, p. 70)

- Researchers may doubt that respondents have read or understood a consent form. Should researchers take steps to ensure that all respondents have fully comprehended the main points of a consent form? How much time should be devoted to that task? Will it alienate or empower respondents? Should consent be solicited only once at the outset of the research? Or, should it be reconfirmed as the research progresses? (Sin, 2005)

- If one member of a family or an organization agrees to participate, is it okay to ask that person questions about other family members? Can a husband, son, or daughter provide information about the mental health (e.g., depression) or substance abuse (e.g., alcoholism, heroin) of the mother without the researchers first asking for the mother's consent? Can one employee provide detailed information about the behavior and attitudes of other specific employees (from whom consent was not sought)? If an IRB requires that permission be sought from all members of an organization, would the research become extremely difficult or impossible to conduct? (E.g., see Borgatti & Molina, 2003).

Because of innumerable gray areas such as these, researchers must select between imperfect options. Whenever researchers collect data directly from human subjects, it is thus possible to raise critical questions about the ethical choices they made.

☆ FINDING IMPERFECTIONS IN RESEARCHERS' ETHICS

To critique the ethics of a journal article, I would recommend searching for authors' *admissions* and *omissions*—that is, focus on what researchers do say and what they do not say about the morality of their methodologies.

Let's revisit Sun et al.'s (2003) article on binge drinking. Recall that the authors distributed paper-and-pencil surveys to more than 1,000 undergraduates at a Southwest university. The only mention of research ethics appears in the authors' discussion of sampling, and can be cited in full.

We targeted a sample size of approximately 1,200 students. . . . Assuming that not all instructors would respond or agree to have their classes participate, we selected 120 classes at random to obtain the <u>instructor's permission</u>. Forty classrooms (about 1,200 students total) eventually participated in the study. . . . The return rate was high because the survey was conducted in the classroom. A total of 1,143 surveys were collected, and 1,105 students were included in the sample after <u>incomplete surveys were removed</u>. (Sun et al., 2003, p. 19; underline added)

Obviously, it would be inappropriate for the researchers to simply show up unannounced at an instructor's classroom and begin to pass out questionnaires without asking permission first. So, the authors behaved ethically by asking for instructors' permission beforehand. And, we can infer from the mention of incomplete surveys that students could choose not to answer certain questions; respondents were not forced to answer each and every item before submitting their questionnaires.

These practices seem ethically sound, but Sun et al. (2003) left some significant issues out of their discussion. For example, the authors do not mention any efforts they may have made to solicit permission from students and not just the instructors.

Keep in mind that the researchers' questionnaire asked incredibly personal questions about drinking habits, legal and illegal drug use, date rape, suicidal thoughts, and family history of drug use, among other issues. It is unlikely, but possible, that a student's responses could fall into the wrong hands—for example, if a completed questionnaire was intercepted by a fellow student or given to campus police. A student's reputation could be harmed, or he or she could be put in legal jeopardy.

Were students told that their participation was voluntary and that failure to participate would in no way effect their grade in the course? Were students told that their personal information would be kept confidential or anonymous? Did students sign a document indicating that they understood that their participation was voluntary and that their information would remain private? What steps did the researchers take to keep respondents' data from falling into the wrong hands?

It is likely that the authors cautiously addressed these matters. Or perhaps not—as readers we can't know for sure.

We do know that the authors were careful about not providing any personally identifying information in their article. No single student was mentioned by name in the article; it is impossible to use the statistics they report to figure out how any particular individual answered any particular item on the questionnaire. The authors protected respondents' identities by not stating which specific courses were included in their sample and by withholding the specific name of the university where the data was collected. Thus, the authors' ethics far surpass the sort of snooping and gossiping that frequently occurs in everyday life. Nevertheless, it is possible that the researchers could have been more careful about collecting and storing data in an ethical fashion.

Now let's revisit Simpson et al.'s (2011) article on power and social networks, which we've discussed before. Like Sun et al. (2003), these authors collected data from students, but they used an experimental design[4] rather than a straightforward survey. One group of students was told to remember

---

[4]An experimental design is one where the researcher manipulates the independent variable in order to better understand its effect on the dependent variable. See Babbie (2010, chap. 8).

a specific occasion when they had power over another person or persons; another group of students was told to remember a time when they were in a low-power position. Then students were given one minute to memorize a set of hypothetical connections—for example, "Mike influences Bob; Doug influences Steve" and so on. In short, the researchers were examining whether being "primed for power" improved students' ability to remember network connections.

Here is the authors' discussion of ethics:

> We conducted two experiments at a large public university with students from Introductory Sociology courses. Those who agreed to participate did so during regular class periods. . . . After all subjects in a given session had <u>read and completed a consent form</u>, a research assistant distributed a packet of materials containing condition-specific information and the dependent measure. (Simpson et al., 2011, p. 167; underline added)

The authors explicitly state that they collected signed consent forms, so we can probably assume that students knew their participation was voluntary and that they could cease participation at any time. The authors do not state whether any efforts were taken to remove any implicit sense of coercion that students may have felt; for example, some students may "volunteer" in the (presumably false) belief that they must do so in order to maintain a good grade in class. Did students who elected to participate receive extra credit in return for their time and effort? And, if so, were alternative forms of extra credit made available for those students who chose not to participate? These are relatively minor ethical concerns, and they may have been addressed by the authors. As readers, we just don't know because the authors don't tell us—not even in a footnote.

For a final example, let's look at two research projects at the same time: one study of a "boot camp" program for violent criminal offenders in Arkansas (Benda & Toombs, 2000) and one study of police officers in Philadelphia (Chappell & Piquero, 2004). In both cases, the researchers achieved a very high response rate—more than 99 percent of their potential respondents agreed to participate in each study. Only 5 out of 600 inmates, and 5 out of 504 officers, declined. Wow—impressive! How did the researchers achieve such high response rates?

In the case of Benda and Toombs (2000), participants were enrolled in a boot camp program that served as an alternative to prison. Inmates who successfully completed boot camp could avoid prison time. About halfway through the program, a staff psychologist (with the help of eight research assistants) administered a 150-item questionnaire to respondents.

In the case of Chappell and Piquero (2004), the researchers attended roll calls at all 23 Philadelphia police districts. Researchers arrived with a list of those officers who had been randomly selected for inclusion in the sample. The ranking officer in charge of roll call (e.g., a captain) assisted in the administering of the survey, which took approximately 15 minutes for officers to complete prior to beginning their shifts.

In each research project, the researchers were dealing with "captive" audiences—literally or figuratively—somewhat similar to students in a classroom. The high 99 percent response rates may be due to the fact that individuals in positions of power facilitated the survey. Thus, I think a critical thinker could raise some ethical questions: Was participation truly voluntary, or did respondents feel pressured by the staff psychologist or by the officer in charge? Were respondents informed that there would be no negative consequences for declining to participate? What steps, if any, did researchers take to shield respondents' information from the eyes of organizational leaders at the boot camp and at the police departments? Were respondents told that these steps would be taken?

Benda and Toombs (2000) and Chappell and Piquero (2004) do not address these types of questions in detail. The authors are largely silent or vague about the nuances of informed consent, along with other ethical issues. This neglect gives the impression that ethics is unimportant or simple rather than a serious issue that involves difficult choices and moral gray areas.

My impression is that such neglect is common in journal articles. For example, J. K. Harris (2008) reviewed 50 articles that collected data from human subjects about their social networks. Only 18 percent of the articles mentioned (however briefly) the issue of informed consent.

Don't simply accept my argument on faith, though. I recommend that you treat ethical dilemmas and the neglect of ethics as matters that you can examine for yourself whenever you read a journal article that analyzes data collected from human subjects. Try Exercise 8.1, and see what you come up with.

CONCLUSION ☆

Virtually everyone could be described as an informal researcher. In the course of our daily lives, we all tend to observe our companions, ask questions, and share personal information with others. Our behavior may be well-intentioned, as when we provide moral support to those going through a period of stress or heartache. On the other hand, people frequently seem to engage in snooping and gossip, seeking out and sharing personal information for the mere titillation it provides.

Researchers also collect highly sensitive information from people, and they share it with others via their publications. However, the purpose of these questions is not to engage in snooping and gossip but to develop better, generalizable understandings of social life. Researchers want to learn, with accuracy, what is going on in the world—and why. They want to develop and test theories and make positive contributions to the literature in their fields but not at the expense of their respondents' well-being or reputations. Consequently, researchers usually engage in a number of ethically laudable practices that surpass those that occur in ordinary human inquiry.

Nevertheless, researchers are not perfect. They make mistakes. They encounter dilemmas with no easy resolution. In their rigorous pursuit of the truth, researchers often neglect to spell out in detail the ethical strategies they used and why they think their ethical choices were the right ones. As a result, even someone who is new to social science—someone with little or no training in research methods—can raise probing questions about virtually any article that examines data collected from human subjects.

EXERCISE 8.1

Read a journal article and look for mentions of ethical considerations.

Do you find these adequate? What potentially important issues were mentioned only briefly or not at all?

If the data was collected by surveying, interviewing, experimenting on, or observing participants, then how was informed consent achieved? Does it appear that participation was voluntary? Could there be any informal or implicit pressure to participate? What steps were taken to safeguard respondents' information and identities?

CHAPTER 9

POLITICS

In everyday life, people routinely avoid conversational topics that might spawn heated disagreements. "Don't talk about politics or religion at the dinner table!" many of us have been told. Movies, sports, the weather, celebrities—these subjects seem much preferred. Keep your controversial opinions to yourself, or else reduce them to a 12-inch sticker affixed to the back of your car.

In the news media, we do hear discussion of important topics. Unfortunately, our national discourse too often seems superficial and uncivil. Politicians debate via slogans, talking points, and *ad hominem* attacks. Pundits on cable television, websites, and talk radio also tend to communicate in aggressive and angry tones—not to mention the rancorous and cruel reader comments that frequently appear underneath stories on websites such as CNN.com.[1]

Social scientists, on the other hand, try to communicate reasonably and calmly, focusing on the rigorous evaluation of theories and data. Scholars dive right into controversial subjects. Anything—poverty, racism, religion, sexuality—is fair game for analysis. Journal articles are not perfect, but they do contain calm, nuanced discussion of serious issues.

I have never read a scholarly paper where one author "yells" at another by using all caps. Can you imagine seeing the following statement in a social science journal?

> In my research I carefully collected and analyzed a data set in order to demonstrate that SMITH AND JONES (2004) ARE IDIOTS!! OMG!

---

[1]There are exceptions to the incivility—National Public Radio can provide a valuable alternative in my opinion. But, in general, popular discourse seems to bring more heat than light to complex social issues.

Instead, journal articles consist of rigorous investigations and reasoned arguments. Once again, I would suggest that research is usually superior to ordinary ways of discussing and learning about social life.

☆ CRITIQUING AUTHORS' POLITICS

Despite the civility and seeming objectivity of scientific discourse, there are some common pitfalls. Scholars are not perfect. They too, are biased. Like politicians, pundits, and ordinary conversationalists, researchers can use cheap debate tricks or subtle rhetorical maneuvers to persuade readers to agree with them (see Gusfield, 1976; Agger, 2000; Knapp, 2002). Even social scientists repeat superficial slogans and engage in subtle *ad hominem* attacks. They too, at times, base their opinions on erroneous information or fallacious reasoning (see Best, 2001, pp. 1–4).

There is much that could be said about the intersection of politics and journal science. However, in this chapter, I will limit my focus to two general questions: How do scholars justify their research topics? And, what kinds of impact might their studies have on the world? These questions can be used to jump-start a critique of the political dimensions of virtually any journal article.

1) How do researchers justify the topics they chose to study?

Writing an article involves making the claim—even if only implicitly—that this topic is important and worthy of readers' time and attention. Very few scholars say, or even believe, that they are writing about trivial topics. Instead, authors seek to draw attention to the topics they find interesting, important, and researchable. Their publications take time and resources: economic support from their universities (or other employers), potential grant support from funding agencies, effort from the peer reviewers and editors, an investment by the journal publishers (who provide copy editing, printing, and distribution), and so on.

Given these investments of time, effort, and money, a skeptical reader can ask: Is this article worth it? Are there other topics that would have been more deserving than the subject the authors chose to research? Arguably, many researchers study topics that can be seen as distractions from more serious issues.

Let's think about some of the biggest problems confronting the world today: global climate change, overpopulation, environmental devastation, the still-remaining threat of nuclear war (e.g., between India and Pakistan). Or, consider the fact that more than 20,000 children die every day around the world due largely to preventable causes related to poverty, hunger, and disease.[2] From the perspective of these dying children and their families, the time and resources that scholars (in the United States and other developed countries) spend on their research often seems misplaced. Do we need to study college students' binge drinking when over a billion human beings lack access to clean water? Terrorism seems like a serious topic, but even that can be debated. Excluding the deaths on 9/11, fewer than 500 Americans were killed in terrorist attacks between 1970 and 2010 (START, 2011).

Authors choose to highlight a particular social problem or set of problems in their articles. But, in doing so, they inevitably ignore and draw attention away from other, potentially more serious social problems. That provides a fairly easy and reliable strategy for critiquing the politics of a journal article. Even if you are overwhelmed by an article's impenetrable jargon and technical statistical analyses, you can raise questions about the subject of the authors' research. Almost any topic can be portrayed as less important than some other issues.

Examining Authors' Justifications

In their introductions and conclusions, authors usually devote a small amount space to explaining why their topic is important. Often, research is portrayed as important simply because it fills a gap in the literature. The research is justified because it provides new insight into a particular phenomenon or advances the state of a discipline or subfield.

Other times, authors provide real-world evidence to indicate that their research topic is nontrivial. Statistics and examples can be used to persuade readers that a serious social problem is being examined. Let's revisit Sun et al. (2003) on binge drinking:

> College students' binge drinking has been considered one of the most serious problems for colleges in the United States. . . . It is estimated that 40% to 45% of college students participate in binge drinking (Haines & Spear, 1996). . . .
>
> The far-reaching negative effects of binge drinking have been well documented in the literature, including: falling behind in school work, physical injuries of self and others, unplanned and unsafe sex, sexual assault, property damage, drunk driving, and secondhand effects of binge drinking experienced by non-bingers. . . .
>
> The purpose of this study is to investigate various theoretically relevant variables regarding their relationships to college students' binge drinking behavior. (Sun et al., 2003, p. 18)

---

[2]See http://www.globalissues.org/article/715/today-21000-children-died-around-the-world, downloaded on October 25, 2012.

Here we see Sun et al. (2003) portraying their research topic as important due to the harm that the practice of binge drinking has. The authors make a compelling case, citing statistics from reputable sources and listing heart-wrenching consequences. Nevertheless, a critical reader could argue that perhaps the problem is not quite as significant as Sun et al. make it out to be. American college students can be seen as a fairly privileged group, much wealthier and healthier than many people in the world. The fact that these students choose to party too hard seems far less important than many other problems—it's a significant issue only when viewed from a First-World perspective.[3] The 1.5 million Third-World children who die from diarrhea each year—primarily because they do not have access to clean water—makes concern over college students' overindulgence seem somewhat trivial and self-centered.[4] The same could be said of research on delinquency, marital equality, terrorism, and many other topics.[5]

My point is that this question—Could the resources (e.g., time, effort, money) that went into a given article have been better spent on another topic?—can be asked of any journal article. Try Exercise 9.1 with a few articles, and I think you'll see what I mean. It's one effective strategy that a neophyte can use to challenge the politics of even the most sophisticated article.

EXERCISE 9.1

Read the introduction and conclusion of a journal article that interests you. Notice how the authors try to justify the significance of their research. Do they focus on their paper's intellectual contributions, on the seriousness of the social problem being studied, or on both?

Compare the significance of the article's topic to some of the world's most pressing problems. Can you make an argument that the research is a trivial or frivolous distraction, given the more pressing concerns that exist in the First World and in the Third World?

---

[3] Go ahead and Google the words *First-World problem* and you'll find a number of websites that make fun of the many complaints of wealthy people. One joke lambasts those who whine about running out of soda or juice: "There's nothing to drink in my apartment (except for an unlimited supply of safe, clean water)."

[4] See United Nations International Children's Emergency Fund/World Heath Organization (UNICEF/WHO) (2009).

[5] Of course, counter arguments to this line of critique can always be imagined. I, for one, believe that social scientists should be allowed to study almost any dimension of the human experience. Extra funding and kudos should go to those who study the most serious problems, but I think almost any aspect of the human experience can be seen as a worthwhile topic of investigation. That said, critical readers should also be allowed to interrogate the explicit and implicit claims that researchers make about the importance of their research.

2) Do researchers maximize or minimize the impact their articles could have?

So far, we've seen that authors can't help but act politically. By drawing attention and resources to one issue rather than another, authors necessarily make a political choice. They have made a moral decision that can be questioned and challenged.

Next, let's focus on a second area where politics intersects with social science: the potential impact that research may have on the world. Even if authors are researching a significant problem, a skeptical reader can question whether an article will make any contribution to the solving of that problem.

In what follows, I'll highlight two issues that can limit the good that journal articles might do: poor readability and weak implications for policy or practice.

Who Reads These Sigh-entific Articles?

Journal articles are infamously dull and incomprehensible. For whatever reason, there seems to be a tension between writing engagingly and writing sophisticatedly. Perhaps authors lack motivation or are poorly trained in composition. Or, perhaps the demands of scientific precision make it difficult to write in an accessible and lively manner.

Reading social science can generate lots of sighs—expressions of boredom and frustration. The more scientific an article is, the more *sigh-entific* it tends to become. Tediousness increases as authors try to be more detailed with their definitions, thorough with their literature reviews, precise with their measurements, descriptive of their sampling processes and outcomes, and technically advanced with their analyses. Rigor leads to *rigor mortis,* as all life is drained out of a topic.

Scholarly articles consist of dense prose that must be read slowly with intense concentration in order to be fully understood. This indicates the expertise and thought that scholars put into their work—a positive thing. On the other hand, the sigh-entific nature of articles ensures that they will have a limited audience and impact.

Articles can be seen as technical reports written by researchers for researchers. Scholars engage in high-level conversations with themselves—a relatively tiny audience compared to the readership of, say, a routine news story appearing on CNN.com. And, given the proliferation of disciplinary and interdisciplinary journals (see Chapter 2) and the thousands of potentially relevant articles that are published every year (see Chapter 4), a journal article may be read by only a small fraction of the (already small) group of researchers who might be interested in it, if they only had the time to read more widely.

Admittedly, there are exceptions. Some articles are read and cited by hundreds of researchers. Some are summarized in textbooks that are read by thousands of students. Occasionally, articles do make an impact on policy makers or practitioners. And, there is a small but growing number of academics who are pursuing a more public approach to research—one that addresses wider audiences and makes a greater effort to bring about social change (Nyden, Hossfeld, & Nyden, 2012). Nevertheless, it seems safe to say that the majority of articles are written for a small audience of likeminded experts, and they reach only a fraction of that intended audience. Thus, their impact is, arguably, very minimal.

Don't take my word for it. Treat the issues of readership and impact as open questions—something to investigate as you read journal articles. Do Exercise 9.2 and see for yourself.

EXERCISE 9.2

Find an article that interests you—one that was written at least five years ago. Use www.scholar.google.com (or another relevant database) to see how many times it has been cited. Then, conduct a regular search on www.google.com to see if the article has been mentioned anywhere. Has it been reprinted in a textbook? Assigned in a college course? Used by a practitioner? Cited on any website, for any reason whatsoever? Perhaps look on Twitter: Has the author's work been tweeted by anyone?

Do Authors Explain the Practical Significance of Their Work?

Authors of journal articles must communicate a great deal of information in a limited number of pages. As we've seen in prior chapters of this book, articles contain definitions, literature reviews, and explanations of measurement and sampling strategies, even before they get to the central task of presenting the findings of the research.

By the time they get to their conclusions, authors may have precious little space to explain the implications of their findings—or why their research matters—beyond adding a bit of knowledge to the existing literature.

For example, Sun et al. (2003) end their article on binge drinking by devoting four sentences to the topic of implications for practice. In one of the sentences, they encourage universities to develop nonalcohol-related leisure activities for students. Another sentence suggests that students could be informed of the risks of binge drinking. These implications seem fairly obvious and are given superficial treatment compared to the 11 pages that were devoted to data analysis and findings. The authors have briefly mentioned potential implications of their study, but they haven't done much to ensure that their article has a very large impact.

Consider the article the article by Simpson et al. (2011), which involved data collected from undergraduate students at a large, public university. Basically, Simpson et al. were interested in whether a person's understanding of who is connected to or influenced by whom is related to the amount of power they have. For example, in a hierarchical organization such as a university, does a college dean have a better understanding of the informal connections between various department chairs and faculty members, or might the dean's underlings have a better understanding of those connections?

In their introduction, the authors give a sense of moral purpose to their research by connecting it to the issue of inequality:

> [If] more powerful actors have more accurate perceptions, this would provide a means through which extant power inequalities are maintained or amplified. On the other hand, if less powerful actors have more accurate perceptions, it would provide one mechanism through which social psychological processes reign-in structurally determined power processes. (Simpson et al., 2011, p. 166)

Yet, in their conclusion, the authors provide no concrete or detailed implications regarding the actions that policy makers or activists could take. Simpson et al. (2011) devote virtually no attention to moral questions such as these: How specifically might their research on power and networks be put to use to reduce inequalities? Do the authors plan to send their work to leaders of organizations, to the general public, or to the media? What good might anybody do with the insights that come from the research? The authors don't say. Their work is basic science rather than applied science. Basic science is important and can lead to important understandings and applications further down the road. On the other hand, much basic science may lead nowhere.

Try out Exercise 9.3 on an article of your choice, and see if you think its implications are hearty, mild, or nonexistent.

EXERCISE 9.3

Find a recent journal article that interests you. Do the authors discuss any implications for practice, policy, or activism? What percentage of their paper is devoted to that topic? Is it merely a passing mention or a serious treatment? Are the implications obvious and underwhelming, or are they instructive and important?

☆ CONCLUSION

In everyday life, sensitive topics are often avoided in favor of the weather and similarly safe subjects. When we are exposed to important issues via television, talk radio, and other sources, the treatment is often superficial and acrimonious, at least compared to social science discourse. Researchers delve deeply into all manner of politically and religiously charged topics, and they tend to do so in a calm, intelligent fashion. Researchers' main goal is to seek the unvarnished truth—to understand what is going on in the social world and why.

Despite their pursuit and appearance of objectivity, social scientists cannot escape politics. In this chapter, I focused on two ways that politics pervades even the most serious scholarship. First, scholars make a moral choice when they decide to commit their own (and their editors', reviewers', and publishers') attention and resources to one particular topic rather than some other topic. Second, by writing their articles in dreary, sigh-entific prose, researchers limit the amount of real-world impact their work could have. Researchers tend to neglect wider audiences in favor of addressing a few likeminded scholars. Moreover, social scientists tend to give short shrift to the practical implications of their research, which minimizes the good that could come from their work. Using these ideas, any newcomer should be able to recognize and question some of the political dimensions of virtually any journal article.

CHAPTER 10

WHY READ JOURNAL ARTICLES— AND THINK CRITICALLY ABOUT THEM?

Journal articles are tough to read. Compared to other activities (like surfing the web), reading social science can be dull. Articles consist of dense prose, sophisticated analyses, and almost no jokes. It can be challenging simply to understand the ideas a researcher is trying to communicate. And then the "pictures"—the figures, tables, and graphs—may offer little help. They can be as complicated as the text that surrounds them.

To make matters worse, several layers of complexity are added when we attempt to read journal articles critically. It's one thing to dutifully absorb an author's message. It's quite another to actively engage an article, carefully examining its strengths and weaknesses. A vigilant reader can find numerous pros and cons pervading every aspect of the research process: conceptualizing the topic, reviewing the literature, measuring variables, taking samples, analyzing data, and addressing ethical and political concerns.

Sometimes, when students learn that research is thoroughly and inevitably imperfect, they ask, "Why should I bother reading articles as they are so riddled with flaws?" They quickly switch from a naïve mind-set—thinking that scientific methods simply lead to the truth; into a cynical mind-set—thinking that all research is pointless.

Let's not do that. Instead, let's stop in the middle ground between naïveté and cynicism—where critical thinking resides (Best, 2001). We need to recognize that research, while flawed, is usually much better than ordinary human inquiry. Social science is never beyond critique, but it has strengths and is a useful enterprise.

In this concluding chapter, I would like to reinforce this message by discussing four reasons why it may be worthwhile for you to learn to read, and think critically about, journal articles.

1) College graduates—and especially social science majors— should know how to find and evaluate primary sources.

Many undergraduates choose to major in the social sciences—psychology, sociology, communication, political science, anthropology, and related disciplines. Other students take some social science courses as part of their general education or as electives.

Usually, students' first exposure to social science is through introductory textbooks. These books are instantly recognizable by their large size, color photos, and expensive price tags. Textbooks can do a good job of simplifying large and complex fields for inexperienced audiences. Authors write accessibly with detailed indexes and glossaries. Sophisticated methodological issues are downplayed, while interesting theories and findings receive more attention.

Not surprisingly—given what we said in Chapter 4—even the largest textbook cannot summarize all the relevant research in a discipline or subfield. Instead, authors shine a light on new research that is compelling and intelligible, and on "classic" works that have been influential or stood the test of time. Textbooks tend to reflect the particular perspectives of their authors—as well as the preferences of editors and peer reviewers (e.g., see Best & Schweingruber, 2003). Rather than providing comprehensive and objective summaries, textbooks offer selective interpretations of fields.

I'm not arguing that textbooks can't serve as helpful points of entry into a discipline. They can. However, at some point, students should have firsthand exposure to journal articles. Journals are where the vast majority of researchers report their procedures, findings, and limitations. In order to understand where new ideas come from, and how fields advance (or fail to), students must venture at least briefly into the scary world of scholarly journals. To encounter social science only through textbooks seems comparable to an English student learning about literature only by reading CliffsNotes or by watching the movie.

If undergraduates—especially (but not only) those majoring in the social sciences—finish college without learning how to navigate a journal article, then their instructors have, arguably, done them a disservice.

2) Learning to evaluate journal articles can make you a better researcher.

Most departments of social science require their majors to take at least two courses in research methods. Increasingly, undergraduates are becoming involved in research—either assisting their professors or designing small studies of their own. Those students who proceed to graduate school take even more courses on methodology and tackle more significant research projects.

Throughout undergraduate and graduate levels of training, students must learn to consume research at the same time as they learn to produce research. The two skills are mutually reinforcing in a few ways.

First, if students can become critical consumers of research, then they can find weaknesses in the existing literature. These drawbacks can be treated as gaps that their own research projects can attempt to fill—which is one of the most common justifications for new research projects.

Second, the ability to find imperfections in research is useful for "interrogating" one's own work as well as the work of others. As students design their own projects, they can better anticipate and address some potential flaws. Moreover, the student can better acknowledge their work's limitations to their readers, which is a necessary component of any good piece of research.

Third, students can pursue their projects with more confidence. If a student knows that numerous flaws can be found in almost any section of almost any journal article, then they are less likely to hold themselves to an unreachable standard. They can admit that their work is problematic and simply do their best to reduce or minimize limitations without succumbing to the paralysis of self-doubt.

Good and bad research is a matter of degree across many dimensions. Fledgling researchers, who are trained in the art of critically consuming journal articles, are better able to understand this and can track their progress as they learn to conduct increasingly better research.

3) Learning to evaluate journal articles can be useful for a variety of careers.

Let's pause and think about the physicians who treat our illnesses. Do we want our doctors to stop learning the moment they leave medical school? Probably not. With each passing decade, their expertise might become out-of-date. Over time, medical researchers develop new understandings of diseases and injuries and create innovative treatments. The best medical practitioners engage in continuous education by attending conferences and trainings and by keeping an eye on the literature in their areas of specialization.

By extension, similar arguments could be made for other occupations. In an ideal world, workers in most fields would attempt to stay current on research that pertains to their jobs. Social workers and counselors would read research on interventions and treatments. Educators would peruse scholarship on classroom teaching strategies and parent–teacher relationships. Lawyers and judges would consult social research that speaks to their cases, whether the topic is employment discrimination, recidivism, or child custody after divorce. Activists, marketing directors, and politicians might read scholarship on message framing in order to craft persuasive arguments. The list goes on and on.

Social scientists conduct research on topics that are relevant to most, if not all, occupations. Students who learn to critically consume research may be better able to "keep their programs and practices current and research based" (Rodriguez & Toews, 2005, p. 99).

Sometimes, employers or supervisors insist that controversial changes in practice are necessary. As evidence, they may cite the opinion of an authority figure, lessons learned from past experiences, or even a scientific study. In these situations, an employee who can find and evaluate the relevant research would be well positioned to enter the debate and sway a course of action. Should employees be allowed to work at home part of the time? Are committees an effective way to make decisions and accomplish tasks—and under what conditions do they operate best? What are some effective strategies for measuring customer satisfaction or motivating employees? These and thousands of other important questions are addressed in social science research.

When it comes to our jobs—where we may spend more than 40 hours a week—the proper proverb is definitely not "ignorance is bliss." Rather, "knowledge is power" may be a more appropriate slogan to live by. And those who can intelligently appraise research may be best able to harness or challenge that power.

4) Learning to evaluate journal articles might prove useful whenever you want greater insight into your life or the world around you.

Our jobs are not the only important parts of our lives. Most of us care deeply about our relationships, communities, country, and world as well. People who have learned to critically consume research have the option of reading rigorous research on anything that interests them—assuming they can walk into a university library to use a computer and consult the stacks.

As we progress through life, we are faced with all sorts of predicaments. From time to time, it might be instructive to read the literature on an issue that confronts you personally. For example, you might want to take a look at recent research on how the state of the economy is impacting college graduates, on communication problems in marriage, on the relative effectiveness of parenting styles, on depression or midlife crises, on retirement challenges, and so on.

Sometimes, a friend or relative may make an obnoxious political or moral argument that seems inaccurate, but you don't know why. A relative may claim, "People who don't want to have children are weird." Or, a friend may argue, "People get what they deserve in life—anyone can be successful if they try hard enough." In cases such as these, reading the relevant literature can give you a much deeper and more nuanced perspective on social life compared to what is found in ordinary conversation. This can make you smarter and give you interesting things to contribute the next time the subject comes up. When the issues are central to your self-esteem or your deeply held beliefs, reading relevant research can provide a calmer and thoughtful voice with less judgment and more nuances. Reading critically, you can distill the theoretical perspectives and findings that seem most sensible to you.

NOT THE LAST WORD ☆

In this book, I have tried to help you cultivate a way of thinking. I haven't given you long lists of facts or concepts to memorize. Rather, my goal has been to convince you to make an attitude adjustment or perform a mental balancing act to find a middle ground between naïveté and cynicism. This mind-set does not accept research findings on faith nor dismiss them as worthless. Rather, it encourages you to ask some challenging questions as you think about a study's weaknesses and strengths.

From reading this short book, I hope you take away a perspective and some ideas that you can use. However, keep in mind that social science is incredibly intricate and diverse. I have glossed over much complexity in order make my writing accessible and interesting.

I recommend—if you have an interest in further sharpening your critical thinking skills—that you don't treat this book as the last word. Instead, consider reading additional texts such as Agger (2000), Best (2001), and Loseke (2013). Take more than the required number of courses on qualitative and quantitative methods. Explore related subjects such as the sociology of knowledge and the philosophy of science. Any course on *epistemology*—the study of how we know what we know—might be fascinating and instructive.

The more you practice critical thinking, the easier it gets—and the more fun as well. Social science becomes less tedious and more interesting if readers can engage and challenge texts rather than dismissing them or meekly acceding to their authority.

REFERENCES

Agger, B. (2000). *Public sociology: From social facts to literary acts*. Lanham, MD: Rowman and Littlefield.

Agrillo, C., & Nelini, C. (2008). Childfree by choice: A review. *Journal of Cultural Geography, 25,* 347–363.

Aksoy, D., Carter, D. B., & Wright, J. (2012). Terrorism in dictatorships. *The Journal of Politics, 74,* 810–826.

Arnett, J. J. (2008). The neglected 95%: Why American psychology needs to become less American. *American Psychologist, 63,* 602–614.

Babbie, E. (2010). *The practice of social research* (12th ed.). Belmont, CA: Wadsworth.

Barnes, J. A. (1972). Social networks. *Addison–Wesley Modular Publications, 26,* 1–29.

Bartkowski, J. P., & Read, J. G. (2003). Veiled submission: Gender, power, and identity among Evangelical and Muslim women. *Qualitative Sociology, 26,* 71–92.

Benda, B. B., & Toombs, N. J. (2000). Religiosity and violence: Are they related after considering the strongest predictors? *Journal of Criminal Justice, 28,* 483–496.

Benin, M. H., & Agostinelli, J. (1988). Husbands' and wives' satisfaction with the division of labor. *Journal of Marriage and the Family, 50,* 349–361.

Berger, P. (1963). *Invitation to sociology*. Garden City, NY: Anchor.

Best, J. (2001). *Damned lies and statistics: Untangling numbers from the media, politicians, and activists*. Berkeley: University of California Press.

Best, J. (2008). *Stat-spotting: A field guide to identifying dubious data*. Berkeley: University of California Press.

Best, J., & Schweingruber, D. (2003). Do sociologists actually use the terms in introductory textbooks' glossaries? *American Sociologist, 34,* 97–106.

Blascovich, J., & Tomaka, J. (1991). Measures of self-esteem. In J. P. Robinson, P. R. Shaver, & L. S. Wrightsman (Eds.), *Measures of personality and social psychological attitudes* (pp. 115–160). San Diego, CA: Academic Press.

Blood, R. O., & Wolfe, D. M. (1960). *Husbands and wives*. Glencoe, IL: Free Press.

Blumer, H. (1969). *Symbolic interactionism: Perspective and method*. Englewood Cliffs, NJ: Prentice-Hall.

Blumstein, P., & Schwartz, P. (1983). *American couples*. New York: Pocket.

Bonjean, C. M., Hill, R. J., & McLemore, S. D. (1965). Continuities in measurement, 1959-1963. *Social Forces, 43,* 532-535.

Borgatti, S., & Molina, J-L. (2003). Ethical and strategic issues in organizational network analysis. *Journal of Applied Behavioral Science, 39,* 337-349.

Brandl, S. G., Stroshine, M. S., & Frank, J. (2001). Who are the complaint-prone officers? An examination of the relationship between police officers' attributes, arrest activity, assignment, and citizens' complaints about excessive force. *Journal of Criminal Justice, 29,* 521-529.

Burt, R. S. (1980). Models of network structure. *Annual Review of Sociology, 6,* 79-141.

Chappell, A. T., & Piquero, A. R. (2004). Applying social learning theory to police misconduct. *Deviant Behavior, 25,* 89-108.

Coakley, J. (2009). *Sports in society: Issues and controversies*. Boston: McGraw-Hill.

Courtney, K. E., & Polich, J. (2009). Binge drinking in young adults: Data, definitions, and determinants. *Psychological Bulletin, 135,* 142-156.

Diviak, K. R., Curry, S. J., Emery, S. L., & Mermelstein, R. J. (2004). Human participants challenges in youth tobacco cessation research: Researchers' perspectives. *Ethics & Behavior, 14,* 321-334.

Erera, P. I. (2002). *Family diversity: Continuity and change in the contemporary family*. Thousand Oaks, CA: Sage.

Fine, G. A., & Kleinman, S. (1986). Interpreting the sociological classics: Can there be a "true" meaning of Mead? *Symbolic Interaction, 9,* 129-146.

Foucault, M. (1979). *Discipline and punish: The birth of the prison* (A. Sheridan, Trans.). New York: Vintage.

Garfinkel, H. (1967). *Studies in ethnomethodology*. Englewood Cliffs, NJ: Prentice-Hall.

Geist, C., & Cohen, P. N. (2011). Headed toward equality? Housework change in comparative perspective. *Journal of Marriage and Family, 73,* 832-844.

Gibbs, J. P. (1989). Conceptualization of terrorism. *American Sociological Review 54,* 329-340.

Gladis, M. M., Gosch, E. A., Dishuk, N. M., & Crits-Christoph, P. (1999). Quality of life: Expanding the scope of clinical significance. *Journal of Consulting and Clinical Psychology, 67,* 320-331.

Goldberg, A. E., Smith, J. Z., & Perry-Jenkins, M. (2012). The division of labor in lesbian, gay, and heterosexual new adoptive parents. *Journal of Marriage and Family, 74,* 812-828.

Gusfield, J. R. (1976). The literary rhetoric of science: Comedy and pathos in drinking driver research. *American Sociological Review, 41,* 16-34.

Haas, L. (1980). Role-sharing couples: A study of egalitarian marriages. *Family Relations, 29,* 289-296.

Haines, M. P., & Spear, S. F. (1996). Changing the perception of the norm: A strategy to decrease binge drinking among college students. *Journal of American College Health, 45,* 134-140.

Hank, K., & Jürges, H. (2007). Gender and the division of household labor in older couples: A European perspective. *Journal of Family Issues, 28,* 399–421.

Harris, J. K. (2008). Consent and confidentiality: Ethical considerations in public health social network research. *Connections, 28,* 81–96.

Harris, S. R. (2000). Meanings and measurements of equality in marriage: A study of the social construction of equality. In J. A. Holstein & G. Miller (Eds.), *Perspectives on social problems* (vol. 12, pp. 111–145). Stamford, CT: JAI.

Harris, S. R. (2001). What can interactionism contribute to the study of inequality? The case of marriage and beyond. *Symbolic Interaction, 24,* 455–480.

Harris, S. R. (2006). *The meanings of marital equality.* Albany, NY: SUNY.

Harris, S. R. (2008). What is family diversity? Objective and interpretive approaches. *Journal of Family Issues 29,* 1407–1425.

Harris, S. R. (2010). *What is constructionism? Navigating its use in sociology.* Boulder, CO: Lynne Rienner.

Henrich, J., Heine, S. J., & Norenzayan, A. (2010). The weirdest people in the world? *Behavioral and Brain Sciences, 33,* 61–135.

Herman, A. I., Philbeck, J. W., Vasilopoulos, N. L., & Depetrillo, P. B. (2003). Serotonin transporter promoter polymorphism and differences in alcohol consumption behaviour in a college student population. *Alcohol & Alcoholism, 38,* 446–449.

Herring, R., Berridge, V., & Thom, B. (2008). Binge drinking: An exploration of a confused concept. *Journal of Epidemiology & Community Health, 62,* 476–479.

Hochschild, A. R. (1983). *The managed heart: Commercialization of human feeling.* Berkeley: University of California.

Hochschild, A. R. with Machung, A. (1989). *The second shift.* New York: Avon.

Hoffman, R. M., & Borders, L. D. (2001). Twenty-five years after the Bem Sex-Role Inventory: A reassessment and new issues regarding classification variability. *Measurement and Evaluation in Counseling and Development, 34,* 39–55.

Israel, M., & Hay, I. (2006). *Research ethics for social scientists: Between ethical conduct and regulatory compliance.* Thousand Oaks, CA: Sage.

Jackson, R. (2011). In defence of terrorism: Finding a way through a forest of misconceptions. *Behavioral Sciences of Terrorism and Political Aggression, 3,* 116–130.

James, W. (1890). *The principles of psychology* (vol. 1). New York: Henry Holt.

Kettlitz. R. E. (2008). Review of *The Meanings of Marital Equality. Gender & Society, 22,* 832–834.

Kleinman, S., & Kolb, K. H. (2011). Traps on the path of analysis. *Symbolic Interaction, 34,* 425–446.

Klendauer, R., & J. Deller. (2009). Organizational justice and managerial commitment in corporate mergers. *Journal of Managerial Psychology, 24,* 29–45.

Knapp, S. J. (2002). Authorizing family science: An analysis of the objectifying practices of family science discourse. *Journal of Marriage and Family, 64,* 1038–1048.

Knudson-Martin, C., & Mahoney, A. R. (1998). Language processes in the construction of equality in new marriages. *Family Relations, 47,* 81-91.

Knudson-Martin, C., & Mahoney, A. R. (2005). Moving beyond gender: Processes that create relationship equality. *Journal of Marital and Family Therapy, 31,* 235-246.

Kokavec, A., & Crowe, S. (1999). A comparison of cognitive performance in binge verses regular chronic alcohol misusers. *Alcohol & Alcoholism, 34,* 601-608.

Kroeber, A. L., & Kluckhohn, C. (1952). *Culture: A critical review of concepts and definitions.* New York: Vintage.

Laumann, E. O., Paik, A., & Rosen, R. C. (1999). Sexual dysfunction in the United States: Prevalence and predictors. *JAMA, 281,* 537-544.

Lee, Y-S., & Waite, L. (2005). Husbands' and wives' time spent on housework: A comparison of measures. *Journal of Marriage and Family, 67,* 328-336.

Lewellen, T. C. (2002). *The anthropology of globalization: Cultural anthropology enters the 21st century.* Westport, CT: Bergin and Garvey.

Lewin-Epstein, N., Stier, H., & Braun, M. (2006). The division of household labor in Germany and Israel. *Journal of Marriage and Family, 68,* 1147-1164.

Loseke, D. R. (2013). *Methodological thinking: Basic principles of social research design.* Thousand Oaks, CA: Sage.

Maines, D. R. (1988). Myth, text, and interactionist complicity in the neglect of Blumer's macrosociology. *Symbolic Interaction, 11,* 43-57.

Michael, R. T., Gagnon, J. H., Laumann, E. O., & Kolata, G. (2004). Sex in America. In D. K. Wysocki (Ed.), *Readings in social research methods* (2nd ed., pp. 159-166).

Nyden, P. W., Hossfeld, L. H., & Nyden, G. (Eds.). (2012). *Public sociology: Research, action, and change.* Thousand Oaks, CA: Pine Forge Press.

Olson, M. A. (2009). Measures of prejudice. In T. D. Nelson (Ed.), *Handbook of prejudice, stereotyping, and discrimination* (pp. 367-386). New York: Psychology Press.

Park, K. (2005). Choosing childlessness: Weber's typology of action and motives of the voluntarily childless. *Sociological Inquiry, 75,* 372-402.

Patterson, C. J. (2006). Children of lesbian and gay parents. *Current Directions in Psychological Science, 15,* 241-244.

Pessen, E. (1992). Status and social class in America. In L. S. Luedtke (Ed.), *Making America: The society and culture of the United States* (pp. 362-375). Chapel Hill: University of North Carolina Press.

Peyrot, M., & Sweeney, F. M. (2000). Determinants of parishioner satisfaction among practicing Catholics. *Sociology of Religion, 61,* 209-221.

Piña, D. L., & Bengtson, V. L. (1993). The division of labor and wives' happiness: Ideology, employment, and perceptions of support. *Journal of Marriage and the Family, 55,* 901-912.

Read, J. P., Beattie, M., Chamberlain, R., & Merrill, J. E. (2008). Beyond the "binge" threshold: Heavy drinking patterns and their association with alcohol involvement indices in college students. *Addictive Behaviors, 33,* 225-234.

Rodriguez, A., & Toews, M. L. (2005). Training students to be better consumers of research: Evaluating empirical research reports. *College Teaching, 53,* 99–101.

Safilios-Rothschild, C. (1969). Family sociology or wives' family sociology? A cross-cultural examination of decision-making. *Journal of Marriage and the Family, 31,* 290–301.

Scheff, T. J., Retzinger, S. M., & Ryan, M. T. (1989). Crime, violence, and self-esteem: Review and proposals. In A. M. Mecca, N. J. Smelser, & J. Vasconcellos (Eds.), *The social importance of self-esteem* (pp. 165–199). Berkeley: University of California Press.

Schmid, A. P. (1983). *Political terrorism: A research guide to concepts, theories, data bases and literature.* New Brunswick, NJ: Transaction.

Schwartz, P. (1994). *Peer marriage: How love between equals really works.* New York: Free Press.

Shelton, B. A., & John, D. (1996). The division of household labor. *Annual Review of Sociology, 22,* 299–322.

Simpson, B., Markovsky, B., & Steketee, M. (2011). Power and the perception of social networks. *Social Networks, 33,* 166–171.

Sin, C. H. (2005). Seeking informed consent: Reflections on research practice. *Sociology, 39,* 277–294.

Smith, A. D., & Reid, W. J. (1986). *Role-sharing marriage.* New York: Columbia University.

Smith, D. E. (1978). "K is mentally ill": The anatomy of a factual account. *Sociology, 12,* 23–53.

START. (2011). Background report: 9/11, ten years later. National Consortium for the Study of Terrorism and Responses to Terrorism. Retrieved December 10, 2012, from http://www.start.umd.edu/start/announcements/BackgroundRep ort_10YearsSince9_11.pdf

Steil, J. M. (1997). *Marital equality: Its relationship to the well-being of husbands and wives.* Thousand Oaks, CA: Sage.

Sun, A-P., Maurer, A., & Ho, C-H. (2003). Predictors of college students' binge-drinking: Experience of an urban university in the southwest. *Alcoholism Treatment Quarterly, 21,* 17–36.

Trafimow, D., Madson, L., & Gwizdowski, I. (2006). Introductory psychology students' perceptions of alternatives in research participation. *Teaching of Psychology, 33,* 247–249.

Ulmer, J. T. (2001). Mythic facts and Herbert Blumer's work on race relations: A comment on Esposito and Murphy's article. *Sociological Quarterly, 42,* 289–296.

UNICEF/WHO. (2009). *Diarrhoea: Why children are still dying and what can be done.* Retrieved December 11, 2012, from http://www.unicef.org/media/ files/Final_Diarrhoea_Report_October_2009_final.pdf

van Brakel, J. (1994). Emotions: A cross-cultural perspective on forms of life. *Social Perspectives on Emotion, 2,* 179–237.

von Schriltz, K. (1999). Foucault on the prison: Torturing history to punish. *Critical Review: A Journal of Politics and Society, 13,* 391–411.

Warner, R. L. (1986). Alternative strategies for measuring household division of labor. *Journal of Family Issues, 7,* 179–195.

Wong, S. K. (1997). Delinquency of Chinese-Canadian youth: A test of opportunity, control, and intergeneration conflict theories. *Youth & Society, 29,* 112–133.

Wouters, C. (1989). The sociology of emotions and flight attendants: Hochschild's *Managed Heart. Theory, Culture & Society, 6,* 95–123.

Yin, R. K. (2009). *Case study research: Design and methods* (4th ed.). Thousand Oaks, CA: Sage.

AUTHOR INDEX

SUBJECT INDEX

⊗SAGE research**methods**

The essential online tool for researchers from the world's leading methods publisher

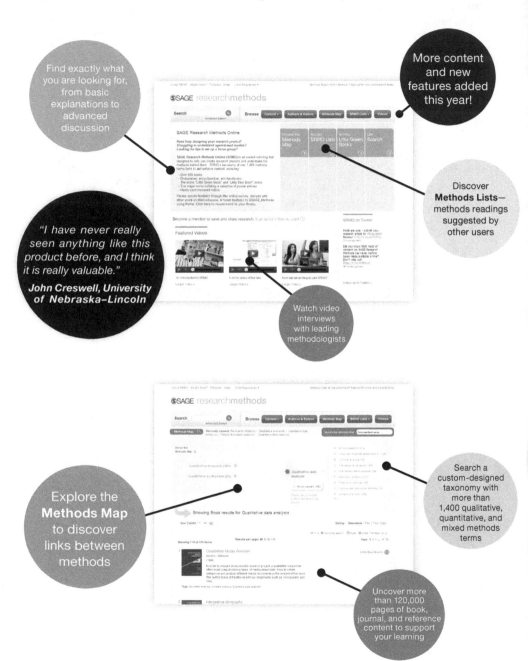

Find exactly what you are looking for, from basic explanations to advanced discussion

More content and new features added this year!

SAGE Research Methods Online

Need help designing your research project? Struggling to understand agent-based models? Looking for tips to set up a focus group?

SAGE Research Methods Online (SRMO) is an award-winning tool designed to help you create research projects and understand the methods behind them. SRMO is a taxonomy of over 1,400 methods terms links to authoritative content, including:

- Over 800 books
- Dictionaries, encyclopedias, and handbooks
- The entire "Little Green Book" and "Little Blue Book" series
- Two major works collating a selection of journal articles
- Newly commissioned videos

Please provide feedback through this online survey, discuss with other users on MethodSpace, or tweet methods to @SAGE_Methods using #srmo. Click here to recommend to your library.

Become a member to save and share research. Sign up for a free account

Featured Videos

An introduction to SRMO · *A demo video of this site* · *How can sociologists use SRMO?*

Discover Methods Lists—methods readings suggested by other users

"I have never really seen anything like this product before, and I think it is really valuable."
John Creswell, University of Nebraska–Lincoln

Watch video interviews with leading methodologists

Explore the Methods Map to discover links between methods

Search a custom-designed taxonomy with more than 1,400 qualitative, quantitative, and mixed methods terms

Uncover more than 120,000 pages of book, journal, and reference content to support your learning

Find out more at
www.sageresearchmethods.com